Synergos

Synergos

Selected Poems of Roberto Manzano

etruscan press

Etruscan Press
Wilkes University
84 West South Street
Wilkes-Barre, PA 18766

W WILKES UNIVERSITY

www.etruscanpress.org

Printed in the United States of America

Publishers Cataloging-in-Publication
Manzano Diaz, Roberto, 1949-
        [Synergos. English & Spanish]
        Synergos : selected poems of Roberto Manzano Diaz /
translated by Steven Reese. -- 1st ed.
        p. cm.
        Translation of: Synergos.
        Spanish text and English translation.
        ISBN-13: 978-0-9797450-1-0
        ISBN-10: 0-9797450-1-2

        I. Reese, Steven. II. Title.

        PQ7390.M183S9613 2008   861'.7
                        QBI08-600239

Designed by Nicole DePolo

Etruscan Press is committed to sustainability and environmental stewardship.
We elected to print this title through Bookmobile on FSC paper that contains
30% post consumer fiber manufactured using biogas energy and 100% wind power.

Etruscan Press is grateful for the support from the
Stephen & Jeryl Oristaglio Foundation, Wilkes University,
Youngstown State University, NEOMFA, Nin & James Andrews
Foundation, Wean Foundation, Bates-Manzano Fund, and the
Council of Literary Magazines and Presses.

The Etruscan Press publication of the present edition
of *Synergos* has been made possible by a grant from the National
Endowment for the Arts.

NATIONAL
ENDOWMENT
FOR THE ARTS
A great nation
deserves great art.

Etruscan Press is a 501(c)(3) nonprofit organization.
Contributions to Etruscan Press are tax deductible
as allowed under applicable law.
For more information, a prospectus, or to order one of our titles,
contact us at etruscanpress@gmail.com.

ÍNDICE

TABLE OF CONTENTS

INTRODUCTION

When Roberto Manzano's selected poems appeared in Cuba in 2005, the book had for its cover illustration a drawing by his son. The image depicts, in the background, the abandoned Tower of Babel rising toward the clouds; and in the foreground—and extending back into the middle distance—a train of human figures walk a road away from the structure, presumably to establish their various communities with their (newly) various languages, and to build what other structures might help them survive in the aftermath of their thwarted, hubristic dream.

As an emblem for Manzano's work in poetry, the image is most apt—first in its appeal to a mythic narrative, an ancient account of our linguistic and cultural dispersal on the planet, with all the grief and glory implied there; Manzano's consciousness as a writer is grounded in myth and the sense that even the most ancient efforts at creation speak directly to us in the present. Second, the image conveys the sense of humanity humbled and scattered, a sense that pervades Manzano's poetry in the form of an abiding sympathy with all people, of all times and places. Finally—and most centrally—the image depicts a chain of human beings walking a road, leaving behind one colossal, collective, and failed attempt at "making," but striding ahead toward other, perhaps more fitting, efforts to give shape to their world. No other images are quite as central to Manzano's *oeuvre* as the road and the traveler, the constant search for meaning, for human dignity, for fitting and forceful modes of expression, for our fundamental connectedness to one another, for our place in the cosmos. It is that sort of journey that his work invites—and challenges—us to take with him.

In terms of Manzano's literary career, that road has been long, trying, unswerving, joyous, and ultimately acclaimed. It begins with *Canto a la sabana* (*Song to the Savannah*), a book of the 70s which did not see publication until 1996, and culminates, for the purposes of the present selection, with the publication of his selected poems in 2005 (though several books have already appeared since then). His list of prizes is extensive, including one for the persistent and illuminating attention to the natural world in his work, and perhaps most importantly the Nicholás Guillén Prize, one of Cuba's highest, for *Synergos* in 2002. His career has also included awards for his work as a scholar and teacher.

Manzano's poetry presents the reader with a great diversity of styles, forms, intentions, imagery, and diction. But even more remarkable than his range is the unmistakable consistency holding the whole body of work together, a consistency born chiefly from two sources. First, Manzano thinks of each book not only as a new effort but an extension of what has gone before, part of a larger cycle of creative activity that joins together discrete poetic acts. Second, the work emerges from a distinctive world-view that makes its presence felt from poem to poem, book to book, a world-view not formed according to any one school of thought but which emerges out of the poet's individual experience and tries to do nothing less than embrace all experience, while at the same time maintaining a humility that acknowledges the utopian character of this ambition. Insofar as there is an "I" in these poems, it is an "I"—as the interview at the end of the present text makes clear—inherited from Manzano's chief influence, José Martí, an "I" that takes upon itself the difficult task of thinking, and feeling, for us all.

Other features of consistency in the work include imagery—road, dust, trees, sky, but also human constructs, machines, tools. Distinctive, too, is the relative absence of personal anecdote or narrative—the poems seem to occupy an imaginative terrain that, if it is sometimes literal, is always symbolic, resonant of energies and synergies beyond the individual. Consistent, too, is the capacious sense of scale, produced at least in part through the play of seemingly opposed forces—dust/sky, suffering/delight, individual/collective, reason/imagination, hope/nostalgia, and others. For Manzano these pairings represent points on a continuum that depend upon each other for their being and for our sense—to the degree that we are able to develop this sense—of the unity of things, of a vastness in which the individual is nevertheless vital.

Which brings us to a final element of consistency in the work, mentioned above, and that is the pervading sense of a shared journey, a mutual traveling through the vicissitudes and raptures of this life, and the firm conviction, established as much through tone and music as anything else, that poetry has the capacity and responsibility to make song of that traveling and thereby to share it with others—including younger readers, for whom the poems in *Pasando por un trillo* (*Along the Trail*) are written. If the departure from Babel represents our linguistic, social separateness, poetry for Manzano represents our determination nevertheless to connect with one another, to find a way to speak to each other and on each other's behalf.

My involvement with Manzano's work began in 2002 when he came to Youngstown State University to read; the poems needed to be translated for that bilingual presentation, and this fell to me. The reading itself was astonishing in many ways, and everyone in attendance felt it; at its conclusion, the substantial audience rose to its feet instinctively and *en masse* to applaud. The current book is the product of that initial energy, and then of an ongoing exchange with Manzano of questions and answers, ideas and explorations, that has clarified the poems in immeasurable ways and increased, just as immeasurably, my esteem for the poet and his work. The critical literature of translation is eloquent about its difficulties, but noticeably less so about its delights—perhaps in the same way that the literature of hell is said to be more interesting than the literature of heaven. When the Spanish philosopher Ortega y Gasset speaks, for instance, of the misery and splendor of translation, one looks forward to the "splendor" passages with the hope that here might be someone who has found a language to convey this crucial dimension of the process; but again, misery steals the show. Of the many delights this project has brought with it, I count as chief the opportunity to get to know Manzano as the writer of these poems. His involvement in their translation has been far more than generous, and my hope is that the translations themselves will speak to my indebtedness to him, and speak of my deep and abiding friendship.

In truth, this book owes its very being to the tireless enthusiasm of my colleague Ivania del Pozo, who first introduced me to Manzano's work, who managed (miraculously) to get him to the U.S. in 2002, who has relentlessly championed his poems, who has written eloquently about them, and who has spent countless hours with me assisting in these translations. I know of no one with more passion and energy for what she loves, in the face of which these poor words of thanks can only be inadequate.

Thanks, too, to Phil Brady and Bob Mooney and the folks at Etruscan for their faith in this project. Thanks to Ana Belén Harris and Ileana Cruz for their help with translations. They and Ivania have weeded out numerous errors and infelicities in my Englishing of these poems; for those that remain, I reserve sole credit.

I am especially thankful to my wife, Kelly, without whose support, encouragement, sound judgment and poet's ear, this project would have foundered.

—SR

AL LECTOR

Todo autor tiene su historia y su prehistoria, como las grandes comunidades humanas. A partir de un instante, signado por un brinco de alguna índole, el modo de escribir cambia, y adquiere ya propiedad para incorporarse socialmente.

Antes de ese giro, del cual se tiene nítida conciencia mucho después, la obra pergeñada debe incluirse más bien en la prehistoria del autor. Aunque es escritura, posee un bajo nivel de estructuración artística. Pertenece a una etapa en verdad ágrafa.

El conjunto de textos que he seleccionado aquí para el lector arranca desde 1970, fecha en que comienza mi verdadera historia literaria, y concluye en 1999, año en que se escribe *Synergos*, mi último título conocido.

Dentro de ese lapso tan largo y tan lleno de vicisitudes vitales y literarias, he escogido aquellas piezas que me parece poseen algún decoro y que pueden ejemplificar de alguna manera mi evolución artística.

De todos modos, el autor piensa que toda muestra mutila ferozmente, y el destino de cada obra es exhibirse y consumirse íntegramente, como mismo fue un día concebida. La integridad del discurso es condición inalienable de la información lírica.

¿Se puede ofrecer con absoluta lealtad una emoción astillada, un sentimiento descuartizado, una cosmovisión entrecortad, como un jadeo o un síncopa? No son buenas las tijeras para los productos del espíritu. Mucho menos para las actividades compactas de la imaginación.

Pero aquí va una selección, a contrapelo de todo lo dicho, con la esperanza de que el lector disfrute los instantes salvados. Desde su prehistoria misma, la trayectoria que hoy se presenta aspiraba a encontrarse con los ojos del lector, cómplice invisible de toda creación, hermano de la inefable aventura.

—RMD

To the Reader

Every author has his history and his prehistory, the way that great human societies do. There's a moment at which, marked by a leap of some kind, the writing changes modes, and takes on the characteristics that make it socially viable.

Before this turning point, seen clearly only much later, the drafted work belongs more properly to the author's prehistory. Though it is writing, it has a low level of artistic structuring. It belongs to what is really an illiterate phase.

The collection of texts that I have chosen for the reader here dates back to 1970, when my literary history proper begins, and goes up to 1999, the year in which *Synergos* was written, my most recent publication.

From that stretch of time, so long and so full of vicissitudes both lived and literary, I have chosen those pieces that seem to me to possess a certain dignity and that can exemplify in some way my artistic evolution.

In any case, the author thinks that any sample is a cruel mutilation, that the end of all work is to be shown and consumed whole, as it was once conceived. Integrity of discourse is the lyric material's inalienable condition.

How can one offer, with absolute conviction, a splintered emotion, a carved-up feeling, a world vision with parts cut away, like a gasp or a syncope? Shears are not a good thing for what the spirit produces. Much less for the unified activities of the imagination.

But here, against all that's been said, is a selection, offered with the hope that the reader enjoys these salvaged moments. Even in its prehistory, the development presented here aspired to meet the eyes of the reader, invisible accomplice in all creation, brother in the ineffable adventure.

—RMD

D<small>E</small> *S<small>YNERGOS</small>* (2005)

From *Synergos* (2005)

(3)

Gusto de ver sobre la mesa ciertas frutas agrupadas como pétalos,
pues ellas saturan los ojos, ávidos del color diverso de la vida;

pero me gusta más ver tu mirada de semilla, tus manos en mis
manos, palpar con mis yemas el ritmo intermedio de tus senos;

sentir el roce de la hermosa fruta de tu vientre, curvada y promisoria,
ese geoide fascinante que ofrece tu cintura;

tu vientre equidista de todo, distribuye arquitecturas deliciosas,
centralidad del mundo, Macchu Pichu del cielo;

desde tu vientre parten expediciones invisibles, los cordeles espumosos
de la gracia, los fósforos fragantes del fervor;

en tu vientre canta la espiral de tu ombligo, cenote de Liliput,
moneda cóncava, ojo primario de la vida;

tu vientre se clausura arriba, se ciñe contra tus vísceras hasta que
es una faja y un gozne de movida elocuencia;

la piel de tu vientre es como una pulida sortija, como una
transparencia de caracol rosado, como un paladar celeste;

hacia arriba tu vientre es solidario y se prolonga en dos colinas
estrábicas hacia donde corre ansiosa la boca;

hacia abajo tu vientre se abre desde el abejeo oscurecido del pubis
en dos litorales donde demorar los labios;

tu vientre es un blando cosechero, todo lo coordina y expande
hacia la edificación soterrada del hijo;

tu vientre zarandea al planeta, como un péndulo líquido,
gira sobre los arranques rítmicos de la entrega;

(3)

I like to see certain fruits grouped like petals on the table, where
they flood the eyes, so avid for living's varied colors;

but I like to see even more your seed-look, your hands in my hands,
to feel with my fingertips the rhythm between your breasts;

to feel the rub of your belly's beautiful fruit, curved and promising,
that amazing geode your waist offers;

your belly equidistant from everything, radiating sweet architectures,
world center, Macchu Pichu of the sky;

invisible expeditions set out from there, foamy strands of grace,
passion's fragrant phosphorous;

in your belly the spiral of your navel sings, well of Liliput, concave
coin, primary eye of life;

your belly closes above, wrapped against your insides like a sash
and a hinge of busy eloquence;

your belly skin is like a polished ring, a shell's pink transparency,
like heaven's palate;

what's above is of a piece with it, an extension in two squint-eyed
hills where the anxious mouth hurries;

and below, your belly opens in the dark hive of the pubis, in two
coasts where the lips linger;

your womb is a tender grower, everything widens and works
together toward this hidden child-building;

it swings to the planet, a liquid pendulum, turns on rapture's
rhythmic beginnings;

tu vientre crece hacia los costados con la misma voluntad de las guayabas, con la misma amplitud de los cometas;

a tu vientre me echo, bajo tus manos de gladiolo, para oír como un indio qué bisontes de ternura trae el horizonte.

your belly swells its sides with a will like a guava's, with a comet's fullness;

I put my ear to your stomach, under your gladiolus hands, to hear like an Indian what bison of tenderness the horizon brings.

(4)

Ahora tengo unas ganas enormes de aullar, oh Munch, de dar un
largo lamento sonoro como una estentórea muralla china;

oh Munch, en el puente que junta los dos cadalsos me sostendría
en la baranda gris para desbridar un gran aullido;

espejo del arte, que guardas el instante raro como una duplicación
absoluta, qué bien cromas lo incoloro;

vertería un ronquido extenso, desenfadado de fauces, de modo que
exhalara de un solo soplo todo el ácido del dolor;

porque ahora exhumo un gran dolor que no es élego ni hímnico, ni
flemático ni atlético, ni femenil ni varonil;

es un dolor, Vallejo, sin sabor ni expediente, hincado como una
mala vértebra en la sucesión congojosa del vivir;

Munch, para un resonar así con los bronquios del alma hay que
poner la baranda, el peso del alma sobre la baranda;

luego que marbeteen, que ausculten, que desahucien como es usual
cuando se ha cumplido la honradez del dolor;

ahora daría un aullido de cíclope, de farallón rocoso, de cristal lan-
zado, de retina pisada, de viento en el desierto;

y no es conmiseración ni perdón ni contribución ni ataque alguno
lo que ahora pido, en vísperas de un gran aullido;

sólo deseo deshabitarme el dolor, como un estertor que de pronto
sale y se divide en dos rostros que se miran de frente;

luego queda el cráter abierto y regresa el aire del silencio dentro de
una inspiración tan larga como un tren;

(4)

Now I feel like letting go with a scream, oh Munch, to give a great
resonant lament like a booming wall of China;

oh Munch, on the bridge joining the two platforms I would stand
on the gray rail to unleash a huge howl;

mirror of art, to preserve the moment as an absolute double, how
well you chrome the colorless;

I would pour out a long rasp, free-throated, so that it exhales all the
acid of pain in a single breath;

for now I'm exhuming a great pain, neither elegiac nor hymnal,
neither phlegmatic nor athletic, neither male nor female;

a pain, Vallejo, without savor or means, lodged like a bad vertebrae
in living's distressing successions;

Munch, to resound like this, with the soul's pipes unstopped, you
need a railing, the soul's weight on the railing;

as soon as they sound and label and declare beyond hope, as is
usual when sorrow's honesty has been fulfilled;

I would let go a cyclopean howl of outcrop rock, of thrown crystal,
of crushed retina, of desert wind;

and it is not commiseration or pardon or contribution or attack at
all that I ask for now, on the verge of a great scream;

I only want the pain to vacate me, like a death rattle that suddenly
comes out and divides into two visages facing each other;

then it leaves behind the open crater and the air of silence returns
in one inspiration as long as a train;

y va entrando, en anillos de tristeza y consuelo, un color de brasa nocturna como una pequeña fiesta íntima;

y disolviéndose el contorno inmediato, ven los ojos aún rojos del resuello las nítidas palmeras de lo distante;

y los grandes alciones cruzan mientras se levanta convaleciendo el sol sobre las pulidas aguas del océano.

it enters in sad, consoling rings, the color of a night ember, like a small, private celebration;

and the world's immediate outlines dissolve, and the eyes, red still from gasping, the eyes see the distance's clear palms;

and the great kingfishers cross the air while the convalescing sun rises over the polished waters of the ocean.

(5)

Así a dónde vamos donde vamos a ir, si necesitamos tanto? Si todo
se gasta un jolongo de algo, un tranvía de eso y de aquello, un triste
diapasón de utensilios;

porque no hay manera, no basta con las manos, no basta con aña-
dir los pies, las rodillas, los codos, los hombros, la cabeza;

no basta: siempre urge una prolongación, un abarque mayor o
menor, una hendidura más larga, una extensión casi planetaria;

en cuanto se viene desnudos y desnudos nos marchamos, debía-
mos tener una desnudez intermedia, pero no es posible;

nos vamos entretejiendo, envolviéndonos, esposándonos, hilán-
donos y deshilándonos, oh Penélope;

y nos vamos alargando, demorando, sucediéndonos repletos de
botones, bocinas, barrenas, oh Odiseo;

grandes son las alforjas de nuestro destino, crecen como los gajos
de un milagro, pues vivimos de adminículos;

dependemos de los artesanos que se especializan, de las industrias
que se especializan, de los países que se especializan;

toda nuestra libertad radica en el aceite, la sal, la tinta, el petróleo,
el papel, el fósforo, el antibiótico;

toda nuestra existencia pasa como un hilo por el que trae el ajo, el
distribuidor hidráulico, el mecánico de las imágenes y los dientes;

oh Edison, cómo es posible? hacia dónde vamos a ir si ya necesitamos
de este modo? hacia dónde, si somos tantos, y demandamos tanto?;

(5)

So where are we going to go, if we need so much? If everything
uses up a sack of something, a tram of this and that, a sad tuning
of utensils;

because there is no way, the hands aren't enough, not enough to
add feet and knees, elbows, shoulders, head;

not enough: always an urgent prolongation, an inclusion larger or
smaller, a longer fissure, a nearly planetary extension;

since we come in naked, and naked we leave, then we ought to have
nakedness in between, but it isn't possible;

we go weaving, wrapping ourselves up, handcuffing ourselves,
spinning and unspinning, oh Penelope;

and we extend, we linger, we succeed ourselves, replete with buttons,
horns, drills, oh Odysseus;

the bags of our fates are large, they grow like the cuttings from a
miracle, and we live by gadgetry;

we depend upon arts that specialize, industries that specialize,
countries that specialize;

our liberty lies in oil, salt, ink, petroleum, paper, phosphorus,
antibiotics;

our existence is threaded through the man who brings the garlic,
the hydraulics dealer, the mechanic of images and of teeth;

oh Edison, how is it possible? where are we going to go, needing
as we do? where to, if we are like this, if we demand like this?

cuántas cucharitas de diversos tipos, cuántos cuchillitos para los
pies, los panes, los pescados;

cuántos espejos y cremas, cuántas tenazas y esmeriles, cuántos
títulos y expedientes, cuántos galones y planillas;

cuántas sogas y diademas, detectores y lentes, armas y bebidas,
aviones y peinetas, espátulas y misiles;

y hemos olvidado los matices simbólicos del cielo, el sabor del
rocío o de la yerba macerada bajo las caderas del amor;

a qué olían las costas de los ríos vírgenes, los langostinos de los
arroyuelos, las manos de la amada dentro de las hojas del sasafrás
solemne?;

fíjate bien, Tersites, que todo es agotable, insostenible, deleznable,
expulsable, pero goza de un acabado perfecto;

fíjate que todo fosforece en líneas puras, pero es para un sólo golpe
de boca o para el paréntesis fugitivo del mes;

qué se fizieron los ebanistas que levantaban aquellos muebles sóli-
dos, aquellas mesas que atravesaban como barcos las aguas de los
siglos?;

qué se fizieron los artefactos solos, que no formaban cadenas de
cadenas, que eran inderivables unos de otros como zafados eslabo-
nes?;

oh Plutón, vivir para tantas cosas grandes y chiquitas, urgentes y
bellas, frágiles y mancomunadas, terminables y extensas;

con cuántos racimos vive el hombre, dentro de qué férulas, árbol
que nunca acaba de gajear hacia la totalidad del viento.

how many various types of little spoons, how many little knives for feet, for bread, for fish?

how many mirrors and creams, how many pliers and emeries, how many titles and records, how many gallons, lists;

how many ropes and diadems, detectors and lenses, weapons and drinks, planes and ornamental combs, spatulas and missiles;

and we've forgotten the symbolic shades of sky, the savor of dew or the soaked grass below the hips of love;

how do they smell, the banks of virgin rivers, the prawns of the small streams, the lover's hands inside leaves of solemn sassafras?;

consider well, Thersites, that everything's exhaustible, unsustainable, weak, discardable, but it has a perfect finish to it;

consider how everything glows in perfect lines, but it's there to be wolfed down, there for the fleeting parenthesis of a month;

where are the carpenters who raised that solid furniture, those tables that crossed the waters of the centuries like ships?;

where are those singular artifacts that formed no chains upon chains, that were unconnected to each other like mad links;

oh Pluto, to live for such things great and small, urgent and lovely, fragile and held jointly, what ends, what goes on;

with how many racemes do we live, in what ferulas, tree that never stops branching toward the totality of wind.

(8)

Yo junto con las manos, con los ojos, con las sienes: siempre estoy
sediento de seres y de cosas, hambriento de verdad y hermosura;

admiro los enlaces, las pitas invisibles, los eslabones finos, los en-
granajes más profundos, las hiladuras más aéreas;

todos los seres y cosas se me asocian en imágenes análogas como
de padre a hijo, como de sobrino a concuñado;

por todos los senderos vienen hacia mis dedos, hacia el iris de mi
corazón, veedor y tejedor incansable, turbinero fragante;

todo se arremolina en mi alma como un vórtice solidario, como un
pozo que circula proyectando espirales sucesivas;

convergencia del oxígeno y del olivino, de las letras y los sentidos,
de los ojos y las almas, de los astros, las yerbas y los bueyes;

padezco una vigilancia enorme, una haladura continua, todo lo
atraigo a los bolsillos de mis versos, al jolongo sonoro;

estoy parado siempre, aunque me desplace, en un pozo a donde
caen los seres y las cosas como las astillas regresando al tronco;

mi corazón crece como un frijol húmedo o un loco mamey procu-
rando nitrógeno y pulpa, fijeza y dulzura;

mis brazos se alargan como ramas delirantes, tienen vocación de
pulpos celestes, de grúa devolvedora del planeta;

me gustan las espigas balanceándose contra el viento, los caballos
galopando por las playas solitarias, el silencio azul de las praderas;

(8)

I gather with my hands, my eyes, my temples; always thirsty for be-
ings and things, hungry for truth and beauty;

I admire the connections, the invisible strings, the fine links, the
deepest gears, the highest threads;

all beings and things are joined to me in analogue images like father
to son, nephew to brother-in-law;

down all the paths they come toward my fingers, toward the iris of
my heart, tireless watcher and weaver, fragrant turbiner;

everything whirls in my soul like a sympathetic vortex, like a well
that circles and sends out successive spirals;

convergence of oxygen and the olivine, of letters and senses, eyes
and spirits, of stars, grasses, oxen;

I suffer a vast vigilance, a constant pull, I draw everything to the
sonorous bag, to the pockets of my verses;

I am always standing, even if I travel, in a well where beings and
things fall like splinters returning to the trunk;

my heart swells like a soaked bean or a mad mamee gathering nitro-
gen and pulp, firmness and sweetness;

my arms lengthen like delirious branches, their calling is to be celes-
tial octopi, or the planet's turning crane;

I like the sheaves balancing against the wind, horses galloping along
lonely beaches, the meadows' blue silence;

me gustan las habitaciones extensas y altas, llenas de páginas y herramientas, de donde salen las sustancias y los pensamientos;

ay, tengo el dolor de los errores, de las culpas, de los tropiezos, de las caídas donde se malogra el destino;

pero tengo también la fe inoxidable, la pujanza del que levanta su lucero del lodo, del que acicala sus propias ánforas;

yo soy rápido de perdón, inválido para el rencor, conmigo puedes hablar como si los dos ya nos hubiéramos muerto;

todo lo junto, lo coso con la aguja de mi esperanza, con la algarabía de seres y de cosas que canta en mi pulso;

me gustan las cornucopias, que acumulan formas, y los relojes, que coordinan funciones;

prefiero la abundancia y el sistema, el desorden de la pasión y de la bondad, la claridad griega de la inteligencia;

todo lo junto con hambre, con sed, dentro de una extraña plenitud que desdeña lo partidario y lo fraccionario;

soy mílite de lo que crece hacia la luz, aunque no sepan los libros y los estatutos responder a ese crecimiento;

me acerco por todos los deltas del espíritu hacia el equilibrio que, como un eje móvil, nos adhiere al horizonte!

I like long, high rooms, full of pages and tools, putting out substances, thoughts;

yes, I am pained by errors, guilts, stumbles, falls where my destiny went unfulfilled;

but, too, I have a stainless faith, the power that lifts its light from the mire, that polishes its own amphorae;

I am quick to pardon, not suited to rancor, with me you can speak as though the two of us had already died;

I gather it all, I stitch it with my hope's needle, with the babble of things and beings that sings in my pulse;

I like the cornucopias that accumulate shapes, and the watches that synchronize functions;

I prefer the plenty and the system, the disorder of passion and kindness, the Greek clarity of the intelligence;

I gather everything with hunger, thirst, in a strange fullness that disdains the partisan and fractional;

I'm a soldier of what grows toward the light, though books and statues don't know how to answer that growth;

I approach through all the deltas of the spirit toward the balance that, like a moveable axis, fixes us to the horizon!

(10)

A veces, con las últimas luces de la tarde, van saliendo poco a poco
de las estaciones los pobres y oscuros trenes;

son metálicos y sucios, atestados de seres presurosos que callan
mientras el silbato se despide de los andenes;

y los postreros trozos de periódicos van corriendo por el cemento,
por debajo de los zapatos, hasta que caen hacia los rieles brillantes;

y entonces, entre la luz sesgada de la tarde, cierta luz de bijol y
aroma triste, se van perdiendo los últimos coches;

y yo soy el viajero, yo siempre soy el viajero, el hombre recostado,
meditabundo, que está parado en el estribo;

soy el viajero que ha partido y que no ha llegado nunca, que busca
lo ilusorio dentro del túnel de los trenes;

y entonces digo adiós a todos, y adiós a mí mismo, y estoy diciendo
adiós, moviendo el pañuelo utópico;

y yo tengo una larga vida detrás, y una larga esperanza delante, y
una opresión dolorosa dentro del corazón que canta mucho;

y a veces soy de nuevo, siempre soy de nuevo aquel niño rural que
veía pasar los pequeños trenes negros de la infancia;

y cómo es posible que yo sea todavía aquel niño, que yo tenga por
dentro el mismo viaje de heridora nostalgia?;

son cosas que no están bien en la evolución de los destinos, porque
duele mucho conservar esa fugacidad dormida;

(10)

Sometimes, with the last light of evening, the dark, ramshackle
trains depart slowly from the stations;

metallic and dirty, crammed with hurried riders who fall silent while
the whistle says farewell to the platforms;

and the last scraps of newspaper scurry over concrete, under shoes
until they fall to the shining rails;

then, in the evening's slant light, a certain bijol-colored and
sad-smelling light, the last coaches vanish;

and I am the traveler, I am always the traveler, leaning back,
pensive, standing down on the last step;

the traveler who has departed but never arrived, looking for the
illusory in train tunnels;

and then I tell everyone goodbye, and goodbye to myself, I am
saying goodbye, waving the utopian handkerchief;

I have a long life behind, a long hope before, and a heart-sorrow
that sings and sings;

and sometimes I am again, I am always again, that country boy who
would watch the small black trains of childhood go by;

and how is it that I am yet that boy, that I have in me the same
journey of wounded nostalgia?;

in the unfolding of destinies these things are not good, there is a
great hurt in preserving that sleepy fugacity;

es mejor ir de coche en coche bromeando con los restantes
ensimismados, con los prójimos distraídos;

es mejor sacar los ojos al paisaje, ya deletreado como un salmo
visual, como una copla monótona;

o hundirlos en las cercas próximas, que van uniendo llenas de prisa
sus postes florecidos, sus muñones negros;

o entrar hacia el alma, viajera lenta, que cruza con sus bártulos
por lo aéreo mientras las chispas de los raíles copian los primeros
destellos de Venus!

better to go from coach to coach joking with others wrapped in their thoughts, with one's distracted fellows;

better to turn your eyes to the countryside, spelled out now like a visual psalm, like a tedious song;

or plunge them into the near fences that rush past, uniting their flowering posts, their black stumps;

or go into the soul, slow traveler, crossing overhead with its things, while sparks from the rails mimic the first glimmers of Venus.

(16)

Bajo la sombra del ilang-ilang
escribo con el sol majado en el mortero del follaje;

allí sentado escribo, en medio del paisaje
interior que los hombres en sus casas se dan;

escribo, mientras los minutos van
cayendo, como mismo bajan las hojas demoradas;

las manos, alertadas,
copian en verbo rápido el suceso;

de cuando en cuando advierto el leve peso
de monedas solares desde arriba lanzadas;

pero la sombra gana la partida
y se siente un frescor que estimula a cantar;

en este manso sitio se puede oír el mar
cuando quiebra su frente en la margen herida;

se podría escuchar la boda enardecida
del basalto y la estrella;

o el texto aquel que dice la querella
—lo cantó Juan Cristóbal—dentro del bosque umbrío;

soy del planeta, pero tengo un fragmento mío
donde poner la huella;

ahora mismo las voces de los que allí trabajan
escucho;

(16)

I write in the shade of the perfume
tree with the sun crushed in the foliage-mortar;

sitting there, I write, in that interior
country that grows in people at home;

I write, while the minutes come
falling the way the last leaf-drift does;

the hands are on their toes
and find rapid verbs for what transpires;

now and then I notice the little sun-fires
like solar coins that the sky throws;

but shadow has the higher score
and a felt freshness, and song is what it urges;

in this gentle place the sea is heard, the surges
when its brow breaks on the wounded shore;

there's a passionate marriage to listen for
between basalt and star;

or that text that says how the limbs spar
—Juan Cristóbal sang it—in the shadowy trees;

I'm of the planet, but there's one piece
of it I call my own, where my footsteps are;

even now I listen to the voices of those
who are working there;

me gusta mucho
sentir cómo el sonido y lo silente encajan;

las raíces que suben, los follajes que bajan
arriban solos a mi copa honda;

soy la cepa y la fronda
de un viejo eslaboneo;

percibo, más allá de lo que veo,
una luz más redonda;

tiene que haber un reino de mayor señorío
y un espacio de más delgada transparencia;

porque lo eterno nace desde la contingencia
y a la cumbre se llega transitando el bajío;

distingo ahora el impalpable envío
de los otros, adentro de esta honda soledad;

siento, por sobre la inconformidad
de mi sangre, una médula posible;

es algo unible
que se columbra hacia la oscuridad;

oh tarde silenciosa,
me siento sin edad, con todo el tiempo unido;

cómo es posible si yo no he vivido
mucho más que la rosa?;

y he sido una centella de carencia imperiosa
y un duro rayo de dolor tremendo;

it gives me great pleasure
to sense, in song, how sound with silence goes;

the leaves that fell, the roots that rose,
alone in my deep glass they are sunk;

I am the frond and the trunk
of a greater light;

I perceive, out beyond sight,
the ancient link;

it must have a reign with vast command
and a space of greater transparency;

for the eternal is born of contingency,
and the summit reached by way of the lowland;

I can make out now what others send,
impalpable, in their isolation's profundity;

I feel, through my blood's nonconformity,
that a marrow can be found;

something to which we're bound
that's glimpsed in the obscurity;

oh evening so silent,
I feel ageless, with all time joined fast;

how is it possible that the time I've passed
is hardly more than what the rose has spent?

I have been a spark of imperious want,
where a tremendous pain's harsh beam burned;

cómo es posible, qué es lo que no aprendo
dentro de esta obcecada lucidez?;

ah la altivez
enarbolada en medio del remiendo;

y no eres dueño
ni de tu propio sueño;

sólo has tenido, y al desgaire,
el aire;

pero has sido monarca del empeño
y de la trémula mensajería de lo invisible;

se te volvió escribible
el mundo;

y ardes profundo
igual que un combustible;

azul derribo, el resplandor ahora
cae trucidado de la altura;

dentro de la blancura
de la página es una rabia invasora;

hacia la sombra protectora
corro el asiento;

y en este movimiento
toco los nudos del espacio;

congruencia viva, todo va despacio
dentro del pensamiento;

how can it be, what haven't I learned
in this relentless brilliance?;

ah the arrogance
that rose up while you were on the mend;

that dream, yours alone,
even that you don't own;

your disdainful share
is only air;

but into a king of persistence you've grown,
and of the tremulous messaging of the invisible;

the world was writable
when it returned;

and you burn
deeply, like a fuel;

blue demolishing, now the brilliance is made
to fall in pieces from a height;

and within the white
of the page an anger invades;

toward the protective shade
I move the chair;

and in that movement is where
I touch the ties of space;

vivid coherence, the pace
of thought slows there;

el discurrir preludia
la idea;

el interés—polea
pertinaz—interludia;

la gana estudia
alrededor;

en la boca la música del verso, ese temblor,
convoca;

y la demanda de seguir provoca
una honda búsqueda interior!

meditation
heralds the thought;

interest—that obstinate
pulley—weighs in;

desire pays attention
to what's around;

in the mouth verse-music, that trembling sound,
calls;

and the demand to go on impels
a searching of that deep, interior ground.

(18)

Voy a salir al mar, a partir atravesando las aguas verdes de la orilla,
las azules de lo alto, a entrar en lo más abierto;

me laceran los muros, los muros, los muros, todos los muros, los
muros propios, los muros ajenos, la letanía de los muros;

el hombre es un animal erigidor de muros, donde se detiene cierra
el aire en torno pidiendo escarapelas y salvoconductos;

un hombre solo está entre sus muros íntimos, cabeceando entre
sus lindes, cercenándose las salidas más amplias;

cuece sus habas silenciosamente sobre el borde ríspido del muro,
como quien descansa a gusto entre sus monedas;

y el más próximo a éste yergue los suyos con sus perímetros vigilantes,
sus demarcaciones belicosas;

y dos juntos ya mampostean apresuradamente, desarrollan sus
instituciones magistrales, establecen los acápites de la ley;

toman medidas de inmediato, que es la agrimensura de los ven-
cimientos, la ingeniería de los éxitos más rápidos;

debemos tomar medidas, así se dicen recíprocamente, alentándose
en el nacimiento brutal de los muros;

y asoman las varas y lazos, y las cartillas donde se resuelve que los
añadidos muevan unánimemente los compases;

y ya en lo alto se ve al guardián gritando: Son las doce, son las
doce!, mientras los sustitutos aguardan debajo;

(18)

I am going to go out to the sea, to set out crossing the green waves
of the shore, the blues above, to enter the most open space;

the walls wound me, the walls, the walls, all the walls, my walls,
the walls of others, the litany of walls;

man is an animal builder of walls, and where he stops the air closes
around asking for insignias, signs for safe-conduct;

a man alone is within his intimate walls, drowsing amid his boundaries,
trimming down the widest ways out;

he boils his beans silently on the raspy edge of the wall, like someone
who rests at ease amid his coins;

and the nearest to this raises his, with their vigilant perimeters, their
aggressive demarcations;

and both together start laying on bricks hurriedly, developing their
masterly institutions, establishing subsections of the law;

right away they make measurements, the surveying of triumphs,
the engineering of the quickest successes;

we ought to take measurements, they say this to each other,
cheering on the brutal birth of the walls;

the beams and the ties poke out, and the cards where it's decided
what extras will have sole charge of adjusting the compasses;

and now up high the watchman cries out: Twelve o'clock, twelve
o' clock!, while the replacements wait below;

y un aire metálico de convicción satura todos los pulmones, dentro
de la nueva parcelación establecida;

se sienten satisfechos de las siluetas creadas, de la resolución para
crear con urgencia unos contornos tan nítidos;

y el mundo se explica bien, porque está sujeto a válvula y plantilla,
a émbolo que tiene su admisión y su escape;

y el olor a muro lo invade todo, como una contaminación que
parece a todas luces indicar la salud de la falsa firmeza;

y yo digo que todos los dedos son prensiles, pero que cada uno
tiene su genio y figura desde de la misma mano;

yo digo que nunca, y en ninguna parte, fueron signo de expansión
los yugos, aunque encuentren bien labrados;

debajo de los muros no nace la brujita ni el baobab, ni puede sen-
tarse el ojo asombrado a escribir un madrigal;

no se puede disfrutar la ligereza de lo redimido, sino padecer un
plomo que se comporta como una losa en el pecho;

por eso yo voy a salir, ya sin lindes, hacia la única linde posible: esa
que se permuta sucesiva en el horizonte!

and a metallic air of conviction saturates the lungs, inside the new established parcelings;

and the stiff silhouettes feel satisfied with the resolution to create, urgently, contours so clear;

and the world is all explained, being subject to the valve and the template, to the piston that has its entry and escape;

and the wall-smell invades it all, like a contamination that seems by all lights to indicate the health of the false solidity;

and I say that all fingers are prehensile, but that each has its own genius and figure within the one hand;

I say that never, and nowhere, were yokes the sign of expansion, though they be ever so well made;

under walls no sorceress is born, no baobab, nor can the astonished eye settle-in to write a madrigal;

nor can the lightness of redemption be enjoyed without suffering a lead plumb that feels like a stone slab in the chest;

and so I am going out, and without borders, toward the one border possible: that which changes endlessly on the horizon!

(21)

Cuando estés sentado solo en la oscuridad final del pasillo no olvides que eres absolutamente indispensable;

no olvides que tú tendiste los jardines colgantes sobre los altos muros, un año tras otro, con tu dedicación solemne;

no olvides que tú has creado la increíble posibilidad anilladora del ojal y del botón, esa divina sencillez;

no olvides que tú erigiste la rebelión simétrica de la pirámide, acarreando quién sabe cómo y desde dónde;

no olvides que tú sumaste ciertas sustancias y las apretaste dentro del portento restaurador de la píldora;

no olvides que tú fuiste probablemente quien aró a Fobos, o quien edificó los tronos que reposan en lo inasible;

y que si no estás allí sentado es porque tú mismo, dentro de la coherencia entre la verdad y el deseo, no lo has querido;

porque si lo hubieras deseado con mayor acuerdo allí estuvieras, de seguro, sentado en los tronos de lo inasible;

pero tú sabes que no lo necesitas, porque allí el aire es inmóvil como en la asfixia de la inmortalidad;

ah, fuiste tú mismo el hacedor, y eres tú mismo el decididor, y ahílas tus días construyendo y escogiendo;

y sólo hacen falta algunas añadiduras, algunos auspicios disponibles, para poder poner en órbita los gestos propios;

(21)

When you are sitting alone in the corridor's last darkness, don't
forget that you are absolutely indispensable;

don't forget that you spread the hanging gardens on the high walls
year after year, with your solemn dedication;

don't forget that you have created the incredible, ringed possibility
of the buttonhole and the button, that divine simplicity;

don't forget that you built the symmetrical rebellion of the pyramid,
hauling who knows how or from where;

don't forget that you combined certain substances and squeezed
them into that restorative marvel, a pill;

don't forget that it was probably you who plowed at Fobos, or who
built the thrones that repose in the ungraspable;

and that if you are not seated there it's because you yourself, in that
coherence of desire and truth, did not want it;

for if you had wanted it with greater accord you would be there,
surely, seated in the ungraspable thrones;

but you know you don't need it, for the air there is motionless like
the suffocation of immortality;

ah, you were yourself the maker, you yourself the determiner, and
you order your days by constructing and selecting;

they need only that added something, some available good omen,
so that the right gestures are put in orbit;

pero tu corazón ha estado lleno de enjundia y sorpresa,
de mucílago y adobe, y en tus entregas te fuiste recibiendo;

y el camino halló tus pies, la distancia halló tus ojos, la gravitación
del mundo halló tus hombros, oh Atlante;

sé que eres, aunque tú no lo consideres, absolutamente indispensable,
que el mundo te reclama, urgido de ti;

porque podemos irnos, pero no podemos irnos, quedarnos es
nuestro verdadero destino de hombres sobre la tierra;

aunque ahora estés sentado en lo postrero del pasillo, con la cabeza
hundida en las manos, mientras cae diciembre en silencio.

but your heart has been full of force and surprise, of adobe and mortar, and in your giving you were receiving yourself;

the road found your feet, the distance found your eyes, the world's gravity found your shoulders, oh Atlas;

I know that you are, though you don't think it's so, absolutely indispensable, that the world demands you, it needs you;

because we can leave, but we cannot leave, staying is our true purpose on the earth;

even though you are sitting now at the end of the corridor, head sunk in your hands, while December falls in silence.

(22)

Enviaré bellas noticias a tu corazón, oh semejante mío, las puliré
como estatuas que capten tus expectativas hondas;

serán recados diversos, todos con orlas y músicas, que irán cantando
sobre el color de la vida mientras das tus pasos justos;

mientras tú vas centrando y orillando tu destino, te llegarán mis
telegramas donde las esperanzas no tienen límites;

todos los papeles que te envío tienen la fuerza del molino eólico,
de la boca terrestre que exhala los cuatro vientos;

no ves esas pequeñas banderas que se suman veloces por la ruta
donde tú esperas que salte la ventura?;

cada vez que nos encontremos te desearé salud y suerte,
desenvolvimiento y paz, la comunión más abundante;

ojalá goces de la carne y el espíritu, tengas silla y fragua,
sepas cómo sostener un colibrí sin riesgo sobre el dedo;

que se te junten los aceites y las cartas, los hijos y los aposentos,
los declives pausados hacia la dicha;

desde aquí te envío una nota, y la veo entrar enseguida como un
bajel colorido en tu corazón de espuma;

son cardiogramas que escribo en la soledad como un cartero
alucinado, oh Cheval, como un ciclista ilusorio;

siempre me imagino que estás en el mismo sitio, que te llegan las
esquelas más tardías, los paquetes más desorientados;

(22)

I will send sweet news to your heart, my fellowman, I will polish it
like a statue that holds what you wait for most;

they will be varied messages, all with borders and music, that will
sing about the color of life while you take your just steps;

while you travel the heart and the margins of your destiny, my
telegrams will reach you where hopes have no limits;

all the papers that I send you have the force of the windmill,
of the earth's mouth exhaling the four winds;

you don't see those little flags gathering quickly along the route
where you hope good fortune leaps out?;

each time we meet I will wish you health and luck, growth and
peace, communion most abundant;

I wish you the pleasures of body and spirit, that you have chair and
forge, that you know how to hold a hummingbird without risk on
your finger;

may the oils and maps be gathered to you, the lodgings, the
children, the slow slope toward happiness;

from here I send you a note and I see it embark right away on your
heart-foam like a colored ship;

they are cardiograms that I write in solitude like an astonished
postman, oh Cheval, like an illusory cyclist;

I imagine always that you are in the same place, that the letters
reach you later, the packages waylaid;

ya no me bastan las caligrafías y las viñetas donde las líneas bailan deseándote prosperidad y adecuado consumo;

qué puedo hablarte de mí que a duras penas enderezo mis gramáticas, que se me pierden las esbeltas gallinuelas;

porque yo me busco de continuo, y siempre reposo sobre la brasa, y soy un eterno estudiante de los jeroglíficos invisibles;

me pongo los dedos sobre el esternón, y siento una alegría y un dolor por mi vida que salgo rápido a enviarte saludos;

desde aquí telegrafío mi solidaridad más vasta, y qué necesitas que yo sueñe por ti, porque yo soy ducho en sueños;

yo tengo una extraña sintonía con lo superfluo, con lo que pisotean, con el ensimismamiento que los otros se callan;

a lo largo de mi vista oteo a las víctimas, y escribo cartas de denuncia que llegan tarde a los altos talleres;

todo se me demora, pues yo soy corresponsal de lo interior, se me va la vida en el polvo fatigado del municipio;

pero para ti, oh semejante mío, estoy enviando desde que nací mis mensajes de lucidez y asombro, de estrellerío insomne!

Ciego de Ávila, abril de 1999

they aren't enough anymore, the letterings, the sketches where the
lines dance wishing you your fill, prosperity;

what can I say to you of myself, who can scarcely get my own
grammar straight, whose railbirds get lost;

because I search myself continually, I rest always on hot coal, I
am an eternal student of the invisible hieroglyphs;

I put my fingers on my breastbone, I feel a joy and sadness through
my life and so I go quickly to send you greetings;

from here I telegraph my vaster solidarity, how you need me to
dream for you, because I am an expert dreamer;

I'm strangely in tune with the left-aside, with what's trampled down,
with the reverie that others silence;

all along where I look I make out victims, and I write letters of
denunciation that reach the high command too late;

everything takes me so long, I'm the interior's correspondent, my
life goes by me in the town's tired dust;

but for you, oh my fellowman, since I was born I've been sending
my messages of wonder and clarity, of insomniac clusters of stars.

Ciego de Ávila, April 1999

De *Canto a la Sabana* (1996)

FROM *SONG TO THE SAVANNAH* (1996)

Salutación Bajo el Cielo

Yo vengo del terrón y vengo de la yerba.
Viento soy en lo alto del molino.
Las reses en el valle se juntan con la noche.
Romerillo de nácar. Rosa de atardecer.
Zarcillo, tegumento, cornamentas, raíces.
Aire abierto, follaje de la tarde.
Intemperie, silencio.
Tierra, tierra, hacia dónde?
Registro con las uñas las raíces,
escucho las semillas cómo crecen.
Trabajadores, vamos a sembrar la aurora.
Ahora, trabajadores, seremos torrenciales.
Y vamos a sembrar el tiempo.
Nos vamos a sembrar nosotros mismos.
Yo vengo del terrón y vengo de la yerba.
Vengo también de sombra cruzando el río.
De verde refucilo en la medalla
insepulta. Clarines que dormitan
bajo las capas húmedas.
Galopan los caballos como truenos rodando.
Silencio. Oye!
Aquí vendremos siempre, de nuevo y siempre,
cada vez que se nuble el firmamento
de la soberanía, aquí vendremos.
Entre los pedregales va cantando la luna.
Susurra su rapsodia la arboleda.
Sobre tu femenino cuerpo verde,
tu tacto de ternura inmemorial,
tus colinas de firme sacramento,
tus arroyos de humilde compostura.
Por entre la luz de tus viejas cepas
y en las veredas rojas de tu sueño.
Con los duros cristales del trabajo

Greeting under the Sky

I come from the earth-clump and the grass.
I am the wind high in the mill.
The beasts in the valley join with the night.
Romerillo's mother of pearl. Rose of dusk.
Vine, husk, horns, roots.
Open air, leaves of evening.
Weathers, silence.
Earth, earth, where to?
I rummage the roots with my nails,
I listen to how the seeds grow.
Workers, we are going to sow the dawn.
Now, workers, we will be torrential.
And we are going to sow time.
We are going to sow our very selves.
I come from the earth-clump and the grass.
I come, too, from shadow crossing the river.
From green lightning in the unburied
medallion. Trumpets that doze
under damp strata.
The horses gallop like rolling thunder.
Silence. Listen!
We will come here always, again and always,
each time sovereignty's firmament
clouds over, we will come here.
The moon sings among the fields of stone.
The grove whispers its rhapsody.
Over your green, feminine body,
the timeless tenderness of your touch,
the steady sacrament of your hills,
your streams' humble bearing.
Amidst the light of your ancient trunks
and the red paths of your sleep.
With the hard crystals of labor

y el reloj incansable de la sangre.
Con los cuarzos azules del destino
y las lajas insomnes de la muerte.
Con las maderas puras de la vida
y los lentos luceros de los trillos,
por sendas de trasiego como un río
vendremos hacia ti, patria mía.
Yo te saludo, patria.
Yo te saludo en nombre de la sangre.
Yo te saludo en nombre de la risa.
Yo te saludo en nombre de los frutos.
Aquí te cito y te congrego
para el canto. Yo vengo de tu lámpara.
Yo vengo del pedrusco y vengo del celaje.
Yo vengo del celaje y vengo de la cáscara.
Yo vengo de la cáscara y vengo de los pozos.
Yo vengo de los pozos y vengo de las yuntas.
Voy hacia los caminos: me voy hacia la espiga.
Voy hacia los cencerros: me voy hacia los surcos.
Voy hacia las faenas: me voy hacia el mañana!

and the tireless clock of the blood.
With destiny's blue quartz
and the sleepless slabs of death.
With the pure lumber of living
and the gradual stars of the trails,
trafficking the paths like a river,
we will come to you, my homeland.
Country, I greet you.
I greet you in the name of the blood.
I greet you in the name of the laugh.
I greet you in the name of the fruit.
I summon and meet you here
for the song. I come from your lamp.
I come from the stone-shard and tinted cloud.
I come from the cloud and the husk.
I come from the husk and the wells.
I come from the wells and from the ox-teams.
I go toward the roads: away toward the grain.
I go toward the cowbells: away toward the furrows.
I go toward labors: away toward the future!

Orígenes

Cuando nos abrazamos, revivimos
otros seres antiguos que se amaron
entre grutas y silvestres racimos.
Los amantes del tiempo se juntaron.

Tal vez en las llanuras de otro día
gente como tú y yo, loca pareja,
rodaron por la yerba en alegría.
Esta dulce locura es nueva y vieja.

Es antiguo el fervor con que te ciño.
Aquí, en mi abrazo, lo ancestral apiño
en oleaje sin linde, como el mar.

Sin estrenar, pasada, ya presente,
detrás de nuestros brazos mucha gente—
tiempo y espacio—se unen para amar.

Origins

When we embrace, we bring back others,
the ones who loved in the distant past
among the caverns and the wildflowers.
The lovers of time were joined fast.

Perhaps on the plains of some other day
another crazed couple like me and you
had their roll in the happy hay.
This sweet lunacy is old and new.

This fervor with which I hold you is ancient.
Here in my embrace the ancestral is blent
in a surge without border, like the sea.

The past, now the present, and the yet to do,
the many who've embraced before us two—
space, and time—in love, a unity.

Canto a la Sabana

A los fundadores del Taller Literario César Vallejo

Buenos días, oh tierra de mis venas,
apretada mazorca de puños, cascabel de victoria.

—Nicolás Guillén

1.
Mi ojo
es un vidrio
negro de presencias.

Recorro la piel y el paisaje de los míos
y los míos se presencian en la corteza.

Desde las raíces
viene la púrpura de la rosa.
Desde la tierra fresca de diciembre
suben los deliciosos cristales de la caña.
Las palmas cantan con el viento
en que habla el espartillo
y en que se rizan las espumas.
Todo se tiende los brazos por debajo,
todo se saluda por encima.
El aire es uno
y una nuestra vida.

Aquí te dejo,
bóveda clara de mi cielo,
este surco de mi arado.
Aquí doy el río insomne de mis venas.
Aquí recojo el calor de las huellas
que los míos ofrecieron a mi sangre.

SONG TO THE SAVANNAH

To the founders of the César Vallejo Literary Workshop

Greetings, oh earth of my veins,
tight cob of fists, small bell of victory.

—Nicolás Guillén

1.
My eye
is a glass
dark with presences.

I travel the skin and landscape of my ancestors,
ancestors present in the treebark.

From the roots
comes the rose's purple.
From the cool ground of December
the cane's delicious crystals rise.
Palms sing with the wind
in which the esparto grass speaks
and the waters ripple.
Everything reaches its arms out below,
everything is greeted above.
The air is one,
and one, our life.

Here I leave you,
clear vault of my sky,
this furrow from my plough.
Here I give the insomniac river of my veins.
Here I gather the warmth of traces
my people gave to my blood.

Soy porque fueron.
El aire está habitado de corrientes,
nunca los caudales se remansan,
y viene el fuego de una mano a otra
como una alegre centella compartida.
Es la invisible población del río,
el rastro de la vida próxima.

Este es el saldo para gustar lo florecido.

Mi ojo
es un vidrio
negro de presencias.

2.
Voy contra polvo,
brumas, espejos.
Voy seguro, queriendo.
Indócil de yemas.
Nazco inmediato de perdigón y yerbajo.
Traigo la memoria, el acicate de su espuela.
El aire verde de la esperanza
repartiéndose en la dueñez del día.
Yerba en primavera,
reventazón del alba.

Ayer no más el chipojo sobre el barro,
reseco de sol a sol.
Ayer no más la brida del bejuco,
los marabuzales del desamparo.
Ayer no más el candil sobre la madera,
el parpadeo mísero de las ventanas.
Ayer no más ciegos como las casimbas,
oscuros como cerrazón de monte.
Ayer no más.
        Y hoy

I am because they were.
The air is alive with currents,
the waters never pool,
and the fire comes from one hand to another
like a bright, shared spark.
It's the river's invisible ones,
a trace of the next life.

This is the price for enjoying what blossoms.

My eye
is a glass
dark with presences.

2.
I go against dust,
mists, mirrors.
Sure, and desiring.
Uncontrollable budding.
I spring from the young partridge and weed.
I bring memory, the prick of its spur.
Hope's green air
shared out in the day's dominion.
Spring grass,
bubbling up of dawn.

Only yesterday the chameleon on the clay,
parched from sun to sun.
Only yesterday the bridle of reeds,
abandonment's thickets.
Only yesterday the oil lamp on the wood,
the squalid flicker of the windows.
Only yesterday the blind ones like deep pools,
obscurities like the forest's dark.
Only yesterday.
        And today

nacen con tanto esmero los días,
ha sido tan preciada y laboriosa la primavera.

3.
He dicho:
Fuera de mis órbitas
todo dujo que alele.

He dicho:
El rosal está en su sitio,
en su sitio el marabú.

He dicho:
Afinamos la pupila
para el milagro de la garza
sobre el anca de la res.

He dicho:
Ciclo solar que no termina,
estamos quedándonos para siempre.
La tierra es esperanza
en la oscura semilla,
espacio y música en la flor,
y luego, pulpa de la vida.

He dicho:
La tierra se ha echado en nuestros brazos.
Junto a la reventazón múltiple,
con ríos en el golpe del pulso,
desbrido el renuevo,
verde de toda la amanecida.

the days are born with such care,
the spring so treasured and painstaking.

3.
I have said:
Outside of my sight,
every bewildering dujo-seat.

I have said:
The rose bush is in its place,
and in its place the scrub-brush.

I have said:
Let's tune the eye
to the miracle of the heron
on the haunch of the beast.

I have said:
Solar cycle without end,
we're staying forever.
The earth is hope
in the dark seed,
space and music in the flower,
and then the pulp of living.

I have said:
The earth has thrown itself into our arms.
I join in the multiple wellings-up,
with rivers in the throb of the pulse,
unbridled renewal,
green with all daybreak.

4.
Toca en este tiple.

Ciñe en tus manos milenarias
este puñado de hierbas frescas,
yérguelas al árbol donde respiras,
tú,
tierra de donde vengo,
donde modelo el polvo de la travesía,
el itinerario sin vertientes,
tú,
tierra a donde voy,
entre algazara y tesón y sueño
y lucero y destello de hojas
y viento que amanece.

Tengo un caudal de sencillos ríos,
de peralejos y sinsontes,
una ronda de sangres,
semejanza pura de polvaredas y caminos.

Toca en este tiple.

5.
Ven conmigo.

Ven a donde afloran, osarios memoriosos,
reconquistadas ya,
las costillas nunca dormidas de mis abuelos,
sus tres inolvidables, la hundida caneca,
el vivaque insepulto, más allá
de la refriega de soles coléricos.
El río, oloroso a tallos de yerba,
a orilla ancestral,
la tierra poblada de brotes,
la sombra de la primera semilla

4.
Play on this small guitar.

Close your ancient hands around
this fistful of fresh herbs,
raise them to the tree where you breathe,
you,
land where I come from,
where I shape the street dust,
the route without slopes,
you,
land where I am going,
amidst din and persistence and dream
and brightness and leaf-flash
and wind that wakes.

I am rich with simple rivers,
with peralejo bushes and mockingbirds,
a sentinel of bloods,
pure likeness of dust clouds and roads.

Play on this small guitar.

5.
Come with me.

Come where the long-remembering bonehouses surface,
reclaimed, now,
grandparents' ribs never sleeping,
unforgettable, the musical instruments, the sunken pot,
the unburied camps, out past
the scuffling of angry suns.
The river, fragrant with grass stems,
with its ancient banks,
the earth crowded with new shoots,
the shadow of the first seed

y el viento joven
vociglero en las frondas.

Ven conmigo.

Tráete los muertos más queridos
que nos instalamos en la vida.

El rebrote solar ondula ya en la yerba,
ya ondula en la yerba

el aire del clarín,
todo a paso de luz al horizonte.

6.
Toca a la puerta
de cada corazón.

No allegues cinchas,
allega espuelas.

No pongas arnés dorado,
limpia la sangre del ijar.

Toca la puerta
de cada corazón.

7.
Me dijo un día
el zunzún de mi garganta:
Qué voces anhelantes te desvelan?
Y repuse yo:
Mi tiempo portentoso
gravita con sus centellas nuevas.
Mi tiempo, raíz devuelta,
es jiquí de la aurora.

and the young wind's
many voices in the fronds.

Come with me.

Bring the dead, the dear ones,
that we may find our place in life.

The sun's return waves now in the grass,
now the clarion air

waves in the grass,
everything stepping in light to the horizon.

6.
Knock at the door
of every heart.

Don't gather saddle straps,
gather spurs.

Don't put on the gold harness,
wash the blood from the flanks.

Knock at the door
of every heart.

7.
It said to me one day,
the tiny hummingbird of my throat:
What yearning voices keep you awake?
And I replied:
My astonishing times
spin with their new sparks.
My times, returned roots,
are the hardwoods of the dawn.

Mi tiempo, romper de lindes,
ajila su sudor y su sueño,
jinetea el crecimiento de los toques más altos.

8.
Sabana,
patria de mis ojos,
desembarazado fulgor;
sabana,
espartillo y corojo en la distancia;
saltanejo,
cielito combo bajo el yerbajo;
palma cana,
movida por los vientos que pasan.
La tierra,
la hora justa de mi tierra,
la sangre insomne de mi tierra,
la brisa garrida y fresca de mi tierra,
es mi legítimo orgullo.

Sabanas de mi patria,
fijas de deslumbre y tersura, altas
en el diapasón risueño de la brisa;
sabanas, las más hondas,
del hombre que las secunda y enarbola,
madera de pura llanada,
labranza segura del futuro.

Sabanas de mi patria,
solares llaneros, ínclitas espuelas,
jáquimas de la vida
asidas para siempre en el puño propio.
Sabanas ya para siempre sonoras,
desde el hombre y desde la tierra,
cosecha de masivo sol y semilla pura.

My times, to break boundaries,
send sweat and dreams marching out,
ride the swelling of the highest chimes.

8.
Savannah,
homeland of my eyes,
unhindered brilliance;
savannah,
esparto grass and tobacco in the distance;
pocked, puddled ground,
skies refracted under weeds;
white-haired palm,
rustled by the passing winds.
Ground,
this very hour of my ground,
the sleepless blood of my ground,
the sweet, fresh breeze of my ground,
is my rightful pride.

Savannahs of my homeland,
steady dazzle and smoothness, highest notes
in the breeze's cheerful scales;
savannahs, the deepest,
from the man who supports and raises them,
wood of pure plain,
sure tilling of the future.

Savannahs of my homeland,
land of the plainspeople, illustrious spurs,
hackamore of life
held forever in the true fist.
Savannahs forever resonant,
from men and from the earth,
harvest of the huge sun and the simple seed.

Casimba de reciente población,
yo sé de dónde te viene la crecida,
quiénes inauguran tus aguinaldos fragantes,
qué nuevos habitantes,
mirada bajo un sombrero venturoso,
galopan tu vasta marímbula.

Sabana,
patria de mis ojos.

9.
Monte.
Voy rompiendo jícaras.
Monte.
Voy entregando espuelas.
Monte.
Voy desenterrando estribos.
Monte.

Que dentro
de mi corazón
en la mañana bruñida
pasan los vivos
con tierras, aires, cielos.

Que dentro
de mi corazón,
catauro sonoro,
apenas con el alba
pasan con su tropa
de cocuyos buenos.

Que dentro
de mi corazón
plantan y fundan
islas con palmas
los muertos.

Hollow so lately peopled,
I know where your waters come from,
who starts your fragrant convolvuli,
what newcomers,
a look from under a lucky sombrero,
they gallop your vast marímbula.

Savannah,
homeland of my eyes.

9.
Woodland.
I go, breaking bowls.
Woodland.
I go, giving out spurs.
Woodland.
I go, digging up stirrups.
Woodland.

Within my heart
in the burnished morning
let the living pass
with earths, airs, skies.

Within my heart,
that resonant basket,
just at dawn
may they pass with their troop
of good fireflies.

Within my heart
let the dead
plant and establish
islands with palms.

10.
Lo que de cuerpo muero
voy naciendo de alma.
A cada celaje que pasa
un muerto me nutre,
un vivo me palmea el ímpetu.

Una tardecita llego y digo:
Este camino de bienvestidos
lo sembré yo.

Llego una tardecita y digo:
Caballo, mancha cerril de la tierra parda,
que galopas como la vida
de la noche al porvenir.

Voy por el surco.
Columbro bateyes transcurridos.
Oteo la senda del horizonte.

En la guardarraya polvorienta y roja
me detengo y digo:
Caramba, qué de raíces caminantes.
Qué cosechas para la luz.

Me detengo en el ateje,
árbol de las uñas labradoras, y digo:
Orgullo,
compromiso de mi suerte,
que sé de dónde vengo y a dónde voy.

Tengo a la distancia de un gesto
el agua,
el lucero,
el jugo de la yerba.

10.
Dying in body,
I give birth to my soul.
With each shade of cloud passing,
one of the dead sustains me,
one of the living applauds my rushing on.

One afternoon I arrive and say:
This road of bienvestidos,
I sowed it.

I arrive one afternoon and say:
Horse, untamed smudge of gray-brown earth,
may you gallop like life
from night into the future.

I go along the furrow.
I glimpse the old sugar towns.
I scan the path of the horizon.

In the dusty red field-roads
I stop and say:
My, what root-travelers.
What harvests for the light.

I stop beside the ateje tree,
tree of the fieldworkers' fingernails, and say:
Pride,
my accord with my fate,
may I know where I come from and where I go.

Only a gesture away I have
the water,
the morning star,
the play of the grass.

Jinete de mí mismo,
he roto los zarcillos antiguos.

11.
Grávida isla,
el mundo nace de ti.

Soy hijo de la yerba que piso,
fecundo su brisa,
ramajeo su oxígeno.

La tierra que me sustenta
me da para el braceo
y para el sueño.

12.
Cuando nací
los mayores me esperaban en el portal.
Dijéronme ese día, llegado apenas:
Bebe de esta jícara,
empínate desde esta racha.
Ve de savia en savia,
rompe los bateyes con que naces
que el cocuyo de nuestra esperanza,
al fin,
        vendrá.
Pasada la noche
no nos olvides,
alcánzanos jirones del amanecer.

Eché piernas por veredas hondas,
cargué con el serón liviano de los muertos,
y era mi sentir lagunato estremecido
por donde pasaban las nubes del día.
Aconteció así
el día que tuve ojos,

My own rider,
I've broken the ancient hold.

11.
Fruitful island,
the world is born of you.

I am the son of the grass I walk on,
I seed its winds,
I branch-sweep its oxygen.

The ground that sustains me
fits me for fathoms
and for dreams.

12.
When I was born
the old ones were waiting for me in the porch.
They said to me, only just arrived:
Drink from this vessel,
rise on this gust.
Go from sap to sap,
break down the mill shacks you were born to
that the firefly of our hope,
at last,
    will come.
When night is done
don't forget us,
bring us shreds of the dawn.

I stretched my legs down the deep paths,
I lifted the large, light basket of the dead,
and it was the trembling pool of my feeling
through which the day's clouds passed.
So it happened

ganas de irme por una ruta.
El día que los mayores,
llegado apenas, me dijeron:
Bebe de esta jícara,
avanza desde esta racha.

13.
Me levanté una noche
y salí a tu aire inatrapable,
sabana.

Quiénes suceden por allí,
briosos de espuelas.
Quiénes, a cuestas la patria,
avanzan por las neblinas.
Quiénes dan su carga inolvidable,
episodian las estrellas.

Salí una noche y me dijeron:
Arriamos para el alba.
Somos el fermento de las raíces,
ya verás nuestra sangre en la llama definitiva.

14.
Sabana vieja,
largo memorial de la patria.
Siempre allí para el trance más difícil,
cumbre invisible del héroe,
muralla pausada de la sangre.
Vigilante y descuartizada
en tus canarreos de fiebre
la patria bajó a levantar su sueño.
Por la bruma de tu lomo
tiñeron el espartillo con avispas rojas
el jinete y su cabalgadura.
Naciendo,

the day I had eyes,
I longed for the road.
The day the old ones,
when I'd scarcely arrived, said to me:
Child of this vessel,
move forward on this gust.

13.
I got up one night
and went out into your uncatchable air,
savannah.

Those who venture there,
with a brio of spurs.
Those who, shouldering the country,
advance through mists.
Those who give their unforgettable burden,
storying the stars.

I went out one night and said to myself:
We're a mule-train hauling toward dawn.
We are the ferment of roots,
and you will see our blood in the final flame.

14.
Old savannah,
the country's long memorial.
Always away and beyond, for what's most trying,
the hero's invisible summit,
slow wall of blood.
Vigilant and slashed
in your fevered channels,
the country fell to raise up its dream.
Through the fog from your back
they dyed the grasses with red wasps,
the horseman and his mount.

apenas en la sombra de la caída,
hábiles para los altos vuelos.

Los héroes esgrimiendo sus claros anhelos,
la tierra más transida.
La contienda en poza de bravura,
espumeante el toro de coraje.
Lontananza. Clarines.
La carga última.

Sabana,
sabana vieja,
la historia naciendo junto a la yerba,
destripando los terrones más simples.

15.
Pongo los pies en tu portal,
tan barrido y fresco,
con este olor de seis de la tarde.

Soy de tu familia,
procedo de tu clara estirpe.
Soy éste que pasa ahora,
que desde su sombrero saluda,
que pone las manos en el agua de tu pozo,
y sigue,
en absorta premura,
los largos terraplenes,
la insaciable sed de la distancia.

...Por los quicios terrosos de mi niñez
cruzaba en silencio el vaho de los caminos,
la alforja y mugre del caminante,
ensimismado en la pérdida de su trillo íntimo.
A las doce en punto,
con plúmbeas botas,

Emerging,
barely in the shadow of the fall,
capable of the high flights.

Heroes wield their clear longings,
the most afflicted earth.
The struggle in a pool of bravery,
the bull of courage foaming.
Far off. Trumpets.
The last burden.

Savannah,
old savannah,
history born together with the grass,
breaking apart the simplest lumps of earth.

15.
I stand in your porch,
so swept and fresh
and smelling of six in the evening.

I'm of your family,
I come from your stock.
I am the one who passes now,
who salutes from his sombrero,
who puts his hands in your well water
and follows,
engrossed and urgent,
the long embankments,
the insatiable thirst of the distance.

…Through the earthy jambs of my childhood
the mist of the road was crossing in silence,
the traveler's pack and grime,
absorbed in the loss of his private path.
Right at twelve,

doblados de fardo,
renqueaban su pesadumbre y su soledad,
venían lacerados por alguna punzada triste.
En el zinc de los portales
hervían los brutales resoles.
Alguna vaca, lela de sol,
orillaba su pesadez insondable.
Y mi niñez a la sombra del platanillo
con unas ganas de sembrar pozos,
regar agua fresca,
poner porrones fríos en las encrucijadas...

Soy de tu familia,
procedo de tu clara estirpe.
Hijeando como plantones
vamos por mi tierra.

Donde quiera me nacen hermanos.
Ahora mismo me llego a tu techo.
Taburetes para mí.
Alborozo de sala. Café.
Rama única,
fruto redondo.
Se anda con ganas de vivir.

16.
En la orilla del recuerdo el sinsonte canta
y es trova tristísima
que deshila la espesura.

La tardecita es fría.
Ulula el viento en la guásima.
Del fondo de alguna gruta
estará saliendo el agua.

with leaden boots,
bent down by their burden,
his sorrow and solitude limped in,
they came cut by some sad ache.
In the zinc porches
the sun's glare was boiling.
Some cow, sun-stunned,
sidestepping his unfathomable heaviness.
And my childhood in the shadow of the large leaves,
wanting to sow wells,
to scatter fresh water,
to put cold jugs of it at the crossroads.

I'm of your family,
I come from your stock.
Sprouting like seedlings
we cross my ground.

Brothers are born to me everywhere.
Even now I am under your roof.
Stools for me.
The living room's joys. Coffee.
One branch,
round fruit.
Then going with a longing to live.

16.
In the margins of memory the mockingbird sings
and it's a grief-stricken ballad
that unravels the thickets.

The evening is cold.
The wind howls in the guásima tree.
From the depths of some cavern
the water will come out.

No me atristo, pero me cae
en ondas hacia lo hondo,
una lluvia difícil.

Y es que en la orilla del recuerdo
el sinsonte canta.

Pero ahora el sinsonte lanza su trino,
monarca de cada vereda,
señor de la tierra cultivada,
y ve pasar en la tarde transparente
las sudorosas camisas
elementales de la victoria.

Ahora las manos y los sueños
vinculan sus impulsos compañeros.
Hilo de manantial
por donde juntas navegan
la leyenda y la esperanza.

Me incorporo en la tierra como un árbol
bajo el fulgor terrestre de la aurora.

Mi ojo
es un vidrio
negro de presencias.

Ciego de Ávila, 1970-1975

I'm not saddened, but it falls on me
toward the depths in sheets,
a hard rain.

And there on the shore of memory
the mockingbird sings.

But now it throws its warble,
monarch of every path,
lord of the worked ground,
and in the transparent afternoon
I see the sweat-soaked elemental shirts
of victory go by.

Now hands and dreams
join their companion impulses.
Thread of source-water
where legend and hope, joined,
sail on.

I join myself to the ground like a tree
under the earthly glow of the dawn.

My eye
is a glass
dark with presences.

Ciego de Ávila, 1970-1975

DE PUERTA AL CAMINO (1992)

FROM *Door to the Road* (1992)

Caminando la Tarde

Derechos van los pinos por la orilla derecha,
rocoso puro, viento blando: anochecerá pronto
sobre la lontananza del camino:
la ropa que traslado con mi hambre
voluntaria está sucia, y busco con los dedos
de los pies raíces, medallas olvidadas,
besos de mujer dulce, los ventanales míos:
está joven mi fuerza, de cumplir la semilla
y fibroso el canto que enderezo:
estoy yo mismo en mi factura propia
y voy como los pinos por mi alma.

Amontono palabras, aprendidas
en cursos de mi sangre, y busco, busco
una que sin raíces desperece el sonido,
alimente clarines, aúpe sus cencerros
y no encuentro sino palabras
de sudor y de lucha ligadas como vértebras
después que el pie atraviesa las espigas.
Así florean, de rabias y ternuras.
Así cantan, de polvo y de silencio.
Así se inscriben, solas de acompañarse tanto.

Ahora quién tuviera un vaso
de buen vino, un mantel abierto
sobre el mundo! Son muchas las palabras,
de cada terrón se levanta el aire
y están los cordajes que se rompen:
un buen vaso, repleto para el himno
dulzón y agreste de la vida! Yo he andado
por los trillos antiguos de mi tierra
extrayendo del jugo de la grama
lecciones modestísimas que se enseñan viviendo:

Walking in the Evening

The pines grow straight along the right bank,
solid rock, soft wind: it will grow dark soon
over the distances of the road:
the clothes that move with my willed hunger
are dirty, and my toes go searching
for roots, forgotten medallions,
a sweet woman's kisses, my large windows:
my strength is youth's, the seed's fulfillment,
and the song I raise up is fibrous:
in what I fashion, I am myself
and stand in my soul like the pines.

I hoard words, things learned
in the courses of my blood, and I search, I search
for one that, without roots, extends the sound,
feeds the trumpets, raises the cowbells,
and I find only words
of sweat and struggle linked like vertebrae
after my feet cross through the field.
Thus they flower, from fury and tenderness.
Thus they sing, from dust and silence.
Thus are they inscribed, lonely from so much self-accompaniment.

Now who would have a glass
of good wine, a tablecloth spread
on the world! There are many words,
from each lump of ground the tune rises
and breaks out in chords:
a good glass, filled for the too-sweet
and wild hymn of living! I have walked
the ancient trails of my land
extracting from the juice of the grasses
the humble lessons living teaches:

ciencia de romerillo, tratado de portal,
conversación sencilla
que en sutiles fragmentos
van hilando los pasos cuando pasan.

Ahora esta simple sabiduría, ahora que acumulo
mis naves, caminando
solitario por entre los pinos, sólo pido
un buen vaso de vino para el alma.

romerillo science, the treatise on porches,
simple conversation
that threads, in subtle fragments,
the footsteps as they pass.

Now this simple wisdom, now that I gather
my ships, walking
alone among the pines, I ask only
a good glass of wine for the soul.

El Hilo

Entre todas las cosas pasa un hilo:
no es de un solo color sino de muchos
y va uniéndolo todo en lo secreto:
cuando te paras, el hilo se detiene
y apenas te encaminas va contigo:
así la flor, la luz del alto día,
a través de la noche, del tiempo y de la tierra,
debajo de tus plantas y encima de tu frente
el hilo te acompaña:
solo, en el borde mismo de la muerte,
con otros, hacia el centro de la vida,
cruzando la avenida populosa
o de pie en el peñón del litoral
entre las hojas pasa el hilo, entre
los miles de calzados pasa el hilo
y pasa de una cosa a otra, pasa
de las cosas a ti, de ti a los otros
y luego de los otros vuelve a ti:
el hilo, simplemente, va en la tierra
coordinando el suceso y la esperanza,
la materia y el sueño, el afán y la dicha
y el hilo te acompaña sin descanso,
te sigue sin reposo mientras vivas
y al caer en la muerte, entonces su color
se ilumina en el borde de la sombra.

The Thread

Between all things there runs a thread:
not of one color only, but of many,
and it unites all things in the mystery:
when you stop, the thread stops with you
and as soon as you set out again it joins you:
thus through the flower, midday light,
through the night, through time and the earth,
under your plants and over your brow
the thread goes with you:
alone, on the very brink of death,
with others, toward the center of life,
crossing the crowded avenue
or standing on a shoreline crag,
between leaves the thread passes, runs
through the thousands of shoes
and goes from one thing to another, passes
from those things to you, from you to others
and then from those others again to you:
the thread, simply, travels the earth
suiting what happens to what's hoped for,
the matter to the dream, the desire to the joy
and the thread goes with you without pause,
it follows without rest while you live
and right to your death-fall, when its color
brightens at the shadow's edge.

NOCTURNO

Entonces en la noche un sonar sin sonido,
audible y aguzado como alfiler sonoro:
se concentran las capas de silencio
y es existencia lo que se reúne: aquí está el lirio
aquel de la ventura, la terrestre azucena
de la nostalgia: todo en melancólico saco
como un viaje o un adiós. He visto que sucede
sin querer, sucediendo.
                    Me recuerdo a mí mismo
en sitios que no son, y sin embargo
convocan roncamente a la tristeza.
          Y es una noche ya lejana que se acerca
desde un camino polvoriento, son ciertas cáscaras
frutales de mi infancia, meteoros en la noche:
vida, vida fugaz:
               se acumulan las hojas
en los húmedos trillos
de un bosque: dónde están las estatuas?
Nadie contesta por la tierra sino es mi propia vida
que se acerca creciendo desde la sombra.
Qué somos cuando somos? Somos tierra, y somos
un trasegar de espigas en el viento,
y un número de gotas
cantando lentamente: pero los granos crecen
juntos en la mazorca, se sostienen unánimes las briznas
y ondulan los potreros bajo el cielo.
               Aquí estoy. Aquí estamos.
Arden, arriba, los luceros. El silencio
se cuaja de colmenas imprevistas.
Ahora bajo un cielo lejanísimo
oigo voces y luces atravesar las puertas de la noche
y es un niño pequeño lo que miro: desde lejos sus ojos
me miran tristemente:

NOCTURNE

Then in the night a sounding without sound,
audible and sharp like a resonant pin:
the layers of silence are gathered
and existence itself assembled: here is that iris
of good fortune, the earthly white lily
of nostalgia: all in a melancholy bagful
like a journey or a goodbye. I've seen what I'd not
thought would happen, happening.
                        I recall myself
in places that are no more, and still
they growl a summons of sadness.
            And it's a night long gone that approaches
from a dusty road, certain peels of fruit
from my childhood, meteors in the night:
life, fleeting life:
            the leaves gather
in the damp trails
of a wood: where are the statues?
No one on earth answers but my own life
approaches, growing out of shadow.
What are we when we are? We are earth, we are
a shuffling of sheaves in the wind,
a certain number of drops
singing slowly: but the grains' growing
joins in the cob, the flag-leaves stand unanimous
and the fields wave under the sky.
                Here I am. Here we are.
Above, the stars burn. The silence
fills with unforeseen hives.
Under a far-off sky now
I hear voices and lights cross the night's doorways
and I am watching a small child: his distant eyes
look at me sadly:

quién eres, niño? Yo soy tú, dice
recogiéndose lento hacia lo olvidado,
imagen demolida que tan sólo abandona cuando parte
una mínima estrella.
   Y después es la noche,
la noche que palpo con mis oídos, solo
como un árbol.

who are you, child? I am you, he says
slowly withdrawing toward oblivion
broken image that retreats only
when a tiny star sets out.
    And then it is night,
the night that I touch with my ears, alone
like a tree.

El Poeta

Me será clausurada alguna puerta?
Entraré. Soy un hombre, simplemente, que canta.
Yo soy aquel que busca por entre la manigua propia,
por entre la manigua de los otros.
En tu sala me siento para decirte:
                          Vives, hermano mío?
No yerro por los trillos
sino después de alzar cada minuto
con otros, entre otros, las tablas de mi puerta.
He cumplido con una porción de mi destino,
y a cumplir vengo con la otra.
Tuve y tengo una vida, y le inscribí un sentido.
Indagaré, al sentarme, lo primero:
                          Tiene sentido tu existencia?
Voy tocando las flores invisibles,
los herrajes oscuros, las serventías de silencio.
Ilustre soy, igual que un carpintero,
aunque trabajo en una alta ebanistería,
de veta más difícil.
                          Guardo los utensilios
y me voy por la tierra, directo a los umbrales.
Estamos esperando tus palabras
tristes o alegres, tus palabras
obedientes al júbilo o la angustia.
Aún siendo tan pequeñas como un grano
de apasote entrarán al ancho río.
Quién le pone medidas a una gota de sangre?
Música de los brazos, de los sueños,
de la muerte, del puro impulso, de la vida.
Aquí, en medio del polvo y del viento,
coloco cada día la silla de mi canto.
Si echas un canto de menos, yo podría hacerlo.
Yo también tengo oficio,
con el cuello sudado y la suela gastada

THE POET

Will any door be closed against me?
I will enter. I am a man, simply, who sings.
I am he who searches his countryside,
who searches the countryside of others.
I sit down in your living room to say:
                    Are you alive, my brother?
I don't wander the trails
without afterwards lifting, each minute
with others, among others, the planks of my door.
I have fulfilled one part of my destiny,
and I come to fulfill the other.
I had and have one life, and I ascribed it a meaning.
I will inquire, on sitting down, into first things:
                    Does your existence have meaning?
I touch invisible flowers,
dark metalwork, the inroads of silence.
I am illustrious like the carpenter,
though I work with lofty woods,
the most difficult grains.
                    I put up my tools,
I walk the earth, I go straight for the thresholds.
We wait for your words,
be they joyous or sad, words
obedient to anguish or jubilation.
Though they be small as a pinch
of goosefoot they will enter the wide river.
Who can measure a drop of blood?
Music of our arms and of dreams,
of death, of the pure impulse, of life.
Here, in the middle of dust and wind,
I set each day the seat of my song.
If you were lacking a song, I could make it.
And I have my duties, too,
with sweaty neck and worn-out shoes

cada día regreso del trabajo
en un claro tumulto.
Pero con entusiasta bondad, en invisible
sacerdocio, coloco la silla de mi canto
afuera, contra el polvo y el viento de la vida.
Hermanos, aquí estoy, para servirles!
Todo: todo es grandioso:
no se avergüencen nunca de las demandas propias.
Yo me siento en la puerta del camino
ofreciendo palabras, yacimientos oscuros.
Gota soy del océano
y en cada gota viva está el prisma del mundo.

each day I come from work
in a total tumult.
But with eager kindness, in invisible
priesthood, I place the seat of my song
outside, in the dust and wind of living.
I am here, brothers, to serve you!
All: all is grandeur:
never be ashamed of your own demands.
I sit in the door of the road
offering words, dark seams.
I am a drop of the ocean
and in each living drop is the world's prism.

DE *EL HOMBRE COTIDIANO* (1996)

FROM *THE EVERYDAY MAN* (1996)

Alto Cielo

Cuando cae la sombra plumón a plumón
hasta que su oscura vestimenta es totalmente descendida
ella aparece en el fondo, estrellada y azul.
Es la noche: amplitud recogida,
espesura, racimo bañado de rocío, humedad
de yunta, oscuridad de vacío
en el momento que toco con mi sangre tu alma:
abrid las puertas, es silencio y extensión!,
y afuera, por debajo—continuado sonido—la yerba
va suscitando el trillo: el párpado celeste
ebrio pasa detrás de presurosas nubes
entre los gajos del ciruelo
y los pechos agudos de las aves
palpitan en los nidos: partid hacia el camino,
es la estrellada vastedad!
Hundidamente, andando a las raíces
voy bajando y es tiempo lo que toco,
es un taller profundo lo que escucho
y es como una cadera sombría
toda la superficie del mundo.
        Y entonces sobre la meditativa
frente, decidme, acaso estamos solos en lo oscuro?
Palpitamos tan solos en lo inmenso?
Infinita y glacial es la noche y adquiere
una profundidad velocísima, y un licor de infinito
se apresura hacia el fondo sin fondo de la altura.

HIGH SKY

When the shadow falls feather by feather
until its dark vestment is wholly descended
it appears at the bottom, starred and blue.
It is night: gathered vastness,
density, flowers bathed in dew, dampness
of oxen, dark emptiness
in the moment I touch your soul with my blood:
open the doors, it is silence and expanse!,
and outside, from underneath—continual sound—grass
stirs the trail: the drunken celestial eye
goes behind quick clouds
amid the clusters in the plum trees
and the breasts of the birds
throb in their nests: head for the road,
the starred vastness!
I sink down to the roots,
descending, and time is what I touch,
the deep workings what I listen to,
and the whole surface of the world
curves like a hip in shadow.
    So then, pondering brow,
tell me, are we perhaps alone in the dark?
Are we throbbing solo in the immensity?
The night is infinite and glacial and takes on
a speeding profundity, and the infinite's liqueur
hurries for the bottomless bottom of the heights.

CÓRPUSCULO

Yo soy también el viaje organizado y loco
del espacio y del tiempo, y debajo de este almendro
donde ahora me siento solo a cantarme una canción
me episodian sustancias que no conozco
y a duras penas tan sólo puedo verlas aguzando los ojos de la mente
tan finos como hendijas cubiertas de centellas.
Y así, poniendo así los ojos, desterrando mis manos,
la voluntad callada, un aire el albedrío,
razono el movimiento cerrado de mi cuerpo,
ahora en este instante qué pasa
dentro de las funciones, en el orbe de los órganos?
Ciega es la dura noche del hombre con su cuerpo
y hace falta ventura para el vivir extenso
y no resuelven nada cuajo de miel o leche de carnera
ni aguzado cristal ni máquina curiosa:
qué soy, cuánto soy, cómo van las cosas?
Así la mancha blanca que sale en la corteza
del viejo limonero, quizá la parda hoja
o acaso un gusanillo que sube silencioso
hasta que con el tiempo va todo por encima
desprendiendo sus pétalos resecos contra el viento:
mucho saben las piedras porque no tienen piel
ni vibran como pulpas cuando andan
y no se tienden para dormir nunca
cuando caen cansados ya los párpados.
Cuerpo soy que distingue, suda, proyecta, admira
con falanges, con ojos, con pelos, con cartílagos
desde un codo hasta el otro,
desde las cejas hasta el duro hueso del tobillo
bajo la rueda lenta de los meses,
sobre el aro acerado de los años:
nací y nací, naciendo cada día
y me comienzo ahora un desnacer pausado.

CORPUSCLE

I am, as well, the shaped and crazy travel
of space and time, and under this almond tree
where I sit alone now to sing my song
substances I don't recognize story me
and with great labor I can just make them out
sharpening the eyes of the mind
as fine as crevices covered with flashes.
And thus, adjusting my eyes so, dismissing my hands,
the will quieted, this caprice an air,
I think-through the closed motion of my body,
now in this instant what happens
inside the functions, in the sphere of the organs?
It's blind, the long night of man in his body,
and needs luck to live broadly,
and a thickening of honey or sheep's milk solves nothing,
nor does sharpened crystal or the strange machine:
what am I, how much am I, how is it with things?
Thus the white stain that appears on the bark
of the lemon tree, maybe the brown leaf
or perhaps the little worm that rises silently
until at last it's everywhere overhead
detaching dried petals in the wind:
stones know much because they have no skin
and they don't tremble like pulp when they move
and they never stretch out to sleep
when their eyelids grow weary and fall.
I am a body that sorts out, sweats, plans, admires
with digits, with eyes, with hair, with cartilage
from elbow to elbow,
from eyebrow to hard ankle bone
under the slow wheel of the months,
on the steel ring of the years:
I was born, I was born, being born each day,
and I begin now my gradual unbirth.

ÍCARO

Asciende al cielo como sube el aire
y ve de lejos tierra repartida
entre un sorbo de gracia, uno de vida
y uno de rápido y voraz desaire.

Qué pasa? Sabes qué sucede sólo
con tu ascenso? No sabes, y si sabes
mucho mejor lo saben esas aves
cuyo golpe pequeño cruza el polo.

Ver la tierra pasar, pero animoso
como una muestra de íntimo poder
y de un vivir más hondo y numeroso.

Hay que subir, subir, subir y ver
en espejo más alto el ancho pozo
donde cuaja sin sueño nuestro ser.

ICARUS

He ascends like air, higher and higher,
and from far off sees ground divided, the strife
within a sip of grace, one part our life
and the other a fleet and fierce desire.

What happens? You know what happens solely
in your ascent? You don't know, and if you do
you know less well by far than those birds who go
beating small wings to fly across the pole.

To watch the earth go its way, but soulful
like a showing of innermost power,
of a living more deep and multiple.

One must rise, and rise, and rise, and see there
in the highest of mirrors the wide well
where it thickens, dreamless, all that we are.

Regresando en la Tarde

Extended los manteles! Ha llegado la hora
fragante de la tarde, y en el río polvoso de la calle
van volviendo los rostros del crepúsculo.
Allá dentro se alumbran las cocinas
y allá dentro hay un oloroso tintineo,
un dulce diapasón de utensilios y aromas.
Salve el sabor, y viva la coral de los manteles!
Aún con las huellas en los hombros
del trasiego, aún con pasos polvorientos,
con los mechones secos por el aire,
están las tinas que brillan de frescura,
se acercan revolando las toallas,
arrincónanse las terrosas suelas
y se destrenza un hilo creciente de deleite
que navega, sin rumbo, bajo las lámparas.
Desplegad los manteles, ha llegado la hora!
Hemos vuelto de las sustancias,
de la vuelta del compás, del sudado
aliento, de la grasa y el rocoso. Hemos vuelto
de paginar maderas, de coser sacos,
de equilibrar papeles, de forjar almas.
Hemos vuelto por todos los caminos
conversando con brevedad, pisando
con rapidez el polvo de nuestro reino.
Nos despedimos en las bocacalles
contra el celeste rojo, bajos los flamboyanes
anchos de las calzadas, y entramos por los barrios
como un ejército que ha concluido su victoria.

RETURNING IN THE EVENING

Spread the tablecloths! The fragrant hour
of evening is here, and in the dusty river of the street
the faces of twilight are returning.
In there, the kitchens are lit
and over in there the waft of dishes clinking,
a sweet scale of utensils and aromas.
God save this savor, and long live the tablecloth choir!
Even with their shoulders still holding the traces
of the day's to and fro, even with their steps still dusty,
with hair dried out by the air,
the tubs are shining with freshness,
the towels flutter close,
earth-grimed shoes are put in corners,
and a growing thread of delight unwinds
and sails, without a course, under the lamps.
Unfold the tablecloths, the hour is here!
We've come back from the substances,
from the turn of the compass, from the sweaty
breathing, from the grease and the rock. We've returned
from stacking planks like pages, from sewing sacks,
from balancing papers, from forging souls.
We've returned along all the roads,
talking briefly, treading
quickly the dust of our kingdom.
We say goodbye in the side streets
against the red sky, under the avenues'
wide flame-trees, and we go to our neighborhoods
like an army fresh from its victory.

El Regalo

Hermosa compañera, todo te lo mereces.
Todo lo tienes tú y todo lo recibes, y cuando vuelven
de tus manos las cosas del planeta
son ellas mismas, no lo son y son
aureoladas de uso, impregnadas de un clima
en que creo. De cuanto existe
busco aquello que pueda llamar mío
para que sea tuyo: no veo más que árboles
y reses y molinos y frutas
y un circuito de espuma detrás de la neblina
y no tengo otra cosa: Toma
una escuadra de bienvestidos en febrero
cuando viene el néctar
tocando con sus nudos de perfume
las persianas: Toma la luna de enero sobre la arboleda
o la lluvia de flores que el viento de mayo derrumba
y entra por la malva humilde, siente
el color de las hojas cuando la lluvia cesa:
Toma, por encima de las casuarinas reunidas en el viento,
la alta estrella sola de la llanura:
He de darte también el rumor del regadío
cuando suenan en medio de la tierra roja
las finas mariposas de acero
y te doy un camino de diciembre
cuando se juntan las familias en las casas
y el aguinaldo y la cáscara de almácigo están fríos
por la aurora, y sobre el trillo de botellas verdes
descansa trémulo el rocío.
Cuanto tengo te lo doy; todo lo que amo, lo que he juntado
día a día, en la sangre, te lo ofrezco.

THE GIFT

Beautiful companion, you deserve everything.
You have everything and receive everything, and when
the things of the planet return from your hands
they are themselves, they both are and are not
aureoled with use, pervaded with a climate
I believe in. In whatever exists
I search for what can be called mine
so that it may be yours: I see only trees
and beasts and mills and fruits
and a circuit of foam behind the mist
and I have nothing else: Take
a grove of bienvestidos in February
when the nectar comes
with its nodes of perfume touching
the blinds: Take the January moon over the grove
or the rain of flowers the May wind hurls down
and enter the damp mauve, feel
the color of the leaves when the rain stops:
Take, above the casuarinas thrown together by wind,
the high, single star of the plain:
I must give you too the murmur of the watered field
when the fine steel butterflies sound
in the middle of the red earth
and I give you a street in December
when families gather in their houses
and the convolvulus and the bark of the almácigo are cold
in the dawn, and on the trail of green bottles
the tremulous dew rests.
Whatever I have, I give you; all I love, what I've joined
day after day, in the blood, I offer you.

El Camino

Andando voy por un camino. Es un viejo camino
de la llanura que amo: sasafrás a la orilla
polvorienta, neblina a lo lejos, plátanos y guásimas
donde asoman techumbres, y mis ojos bebiendo silenciosos
la extendida copa: ya pasó
la hora del brindis, la hora agreste y dulce
cuando salí con una ramilla de copal
y una marímbula de puerta en puerta.
Entonces era entonces,
y avanzaba listo a escriturar el viento,
y cuando encendía los cocuyos
se juntaban los míos
debajo del portal con un himno de arcilla cada uno
entre los dientes, con sílabas de fuego,
con lumbres de sudor y sangre.
Me lo entregaron todo y lo elevé en mis puños,
regándolo en el viento de la vida.
Hoy, andando el antiguo camino, he descubierto
como entonces las voces viejas, los nuevos himnos.
Siempre voy por un trillo, y oigo siempre
palabras en la sangre. No está en curso
sino soltar hilillos de música cerrada.
Yo adelanto hacia donde azulea mi sangre
mientras escucho el sasafrás saludarme en la orilla.

The Road

I am walking down a road. It's an old road
in the plains that I love: sassafras at the dusty
edges, mist in the distance, plantain and guásima trees
where the rooftops show, and my eyes drinking silently
from the offered glass: the time for toasts
is past already, the sweet and country time
when I went out with a small copal branch
and a marímbula from door to door.
Then was then,
and I went forward ready to write the wind,
and when I lit my firefly eyes
my family gathered
in the porch with a hymn of clay in their mouths,
each one, with syllables of fire,
flames of sweat and blood.
They handed me everything, and I raised it in my fists,
scattering it to the wind of life.
Today, walking the old road, I've discovered
as then the old voices, the new hymns.
Always I'm going along a trail, and hear always
words in the blood. And always my going
sets little threads of closed-off music free.
I go toward where my blood is a blue distance
while I hear the sassafras greet me from the shoulder.

AGRADECE AHORA

Un día vuelto sobre su explanada
propia, qué ves dónde ves? No ves el trillo
de trizaduras verdes, los ojos de los peces,
las curvas en el aire de la estatua?
No escuchas un silencio, un obstinado estruendo?
Cuando cierran los árboles
la gran circulación de su volumen verde
adentro están las yemas, y luego están los frutos:
ocurre—es la vida—y abajo tal vez hay un niño
rompiendo almendras, y sube el olor seco y dulce
de la infancia, y afuera, bajo el sol,
son camisas y blusas sudadas de la estirpe
llenándose de querencia y voz:s
grábalas en tus ojos que afila el tiempo,
cadenas espumosas que tejen las pisadas
y eres sólo eso: un vivo montículo, un movido
acumularse, y cada ramilla que sonó
te hizo matojo, árbol luego, de dónde vas a venir
si no vienes de otros, de los otros, de todos?
Agradece ahora, que es tiempo, y suma los tablones
acordelando tus materias:
dentro del luminoso espacio reúne las piedras
de tu sencillo monumento. Porque para qué pasas
cuando pasas? Febril e inexorable pasas
y sólo vives cuando sumas tus aguas en el río.

GRATEFUL NOW

The contents of a day turned out on their stretch
of ground, what do you see where you see? Not the trail
of green fragments, the eyes of fish,
not the statue's curves in the air?
You don't hear a silence, a stubborn din?
When the turning, green
volume of the trees closes overhead,
within are the seeds, and then fruit:
it happens—it's living—and below sometimes is a child
cracking almonds, and the dry, sweet smell
of childhood rises, and outside, under the sun,
a bloodline's sweaty blouses and shirts
swelling with place and voice:
record them with eyes time has sharpened,
wave on wave weaving your footsteps
and you are only that: a living mound, a restless
mass, and each twig that sounded
made you a low shrub, then tree, from where will you come
if you don't come from another, others, everything?
Be grateful now, it is time, and put together the planks
as they suit your subjects:
in the luminous space gather the stones
of your simple monument: for what do you pass
when you pass? Hectic and inexorable you go by
and you live only when you add your waters to the river's.

El Trabajo Gustoso

…el trabajo gustoso
                    —J. R. Jiménez

Me senté un día y otro día a escribir como quien vuelve del tráfago
a escoger almendras. Era una labor de fuego y de silencio, viendo
sobre la piedra pulida cómo crecían los gérmenes o se aposentaban
las últimas estrellas. Supuse que era dueño de racimos sin mirar, de
ser tan mirados. He venido sobre la tierra con la alforja con que todo
lo vivo se desliza y permanece, y me dediqué a saturarla a cada paso
viendo con bondad las raíces, los cometas, los ojos y las sombras.
Cómo puedo llenarla con la luz desplazada por mi sola vida si no voy
con detenimiento tocando todas las luces, registrando todas las arci-
llas, acopiando las miradas y enseres? Soy recolector. Produzco con
tanto ámbitos y semillas. Pero al sentarme sobre mi piedra de canto
escojo mi propia flauta, organizo a mi propio modo los bucinadores
de la sangre. Es tan largo el río como una vena cósmica y hay reco-
dos para todos. Yo estoy en mi sitio, y desde él te brindo estos peces
que capturo en la sombra.

Me senté un día y otro día a escribir como quien no tiene más que
una piedra para tallar la piedra. Toqué en la puerta de los muertos
que habían escrito, indagando los hilos y ademanes. Fue mejor que
ir a ver a los vivos, pues siempre volví decepcionado. Qué podían
decirme si permanecían silenciosos, maldiciendo o mirando de reojo
como animales desplazados? Me fui a ver a los muertos y debajo de
lo escrito, levantándolo como una losa, vi cómo tomaban el buril o
la espátula, vi dónde cayó el cincel con fuerza o dónde se dejaron
llevar como el agua de lluvia hacia las más escondidas raíces.

Me senté un día y otro día después de haber hundido el pie en el
lodo, de pisar escamas azules, de ceñir unas caderas movidas por el
cielo, de asomarme a los barandales de la noche. Después de juntar

THE PLEASING LABOR

...the pleasing labor
—J. R. Jiménez

I sat down one day and then another to write like someone come back from the bustle of selecting almonds. It was a labor of fire and silence, seeing on the polished stone the way the seeds grew or the last stars took up their lodgings. I supposed I was the master of flowering branches without looking, from their being so looked-at. I've come crossing the earth with the saddlebag with which the living slip away and remain, and I devoted myself with each step of kindness to loading it with roots, comets, eyes, and shadows. How can I fill it with the light my one life displaces if I'm not careful to touch all lights, searching all the clay, gathering glances and tools. I collect. And with so much, I produce fields and seeds. But sitting on my stone of song I choose my own flute, shape in my own way the embouchure of the blood. It is so large, the river, like a cosmic vein, and there are bends for everyone. I am in my place, and from it I offer you these fish that I capture in the shadow.

I sat down one day and then another to write like someone who has only a stone to sculpt stone. I knocked on the door of the dead who had written, inquiring after threads and gestures. It was better than seeking out the living, from whom I always returned disappointed. What could they tell me if they stayed silent, cursing or looking out the corners of their eyes like displaced animals. I went to see the dead and underneath what was written, raising it like a flagstone, I saw how they took the engraving tool or putty knife, I saw where the chisel struck or where they let themselves run like rain water toward the most secret roots.

I sat down one day and then another, having sunk my foot in the mud, stepping on blue scales, wrapping around hips moving through

monedas o cargar los hijos, de suplir las carencias o contener los desbordes, después de cuanto ocurre me senté sobre la piedra para el canto. Siempre fue después, como una labor olvidada o un gesto de absoluto patrimonio. Nadie vino a entusiasmarme, a ver qué te hace falta, cómo van las cosas. Iba de clandestina mi mejor persona; de arrinconada, mi humanidad más ancha. Pero yo sostuve cada día, sin olvidarme, las lajas del silencio, golpeé contra las lajas hasta obtener la chispa, derramé lo reunido cada día en la oscura vasija. Yo soy soldado de una milicia invisible y no desertaré jamás. A su momento tocaré en los umbrales: He aquí, hermanos, lo que os dejo. Fue en silencio, y después de todo. Donde ustedes estuvieron, yo estuve; como ustedes se hilaron, me hilé yo; yo volví, cuando ustedes volvieron. Y luego me senté en la sombra a esculpir en silencio y solo estas tablillas de barro.

La Guérnica, 1983-1988

sky, leaning over the railings of the night. After gathering coins or carrying children, after filling some need or containing the overflow, after whatever happens I sat down on the stone to sing. It was always after, like a forgotten labor or a gesture of absolute inheritance. No one came to spur me on, to see what you need, how things are going. My better self went secretly; it set things aside, my wider humanity. But each day I held up, without forgetting, the stones of silence, struck them until I got a spark, poured out what was gathered each day into the dark vessel. I am a soldier of an invisible militia and I will never desert. In time I will touch the thresholds: Herein, brothers, is what I leave you. It was in silence, and came after everything. Where you were, I was; as you were spun, so was I; I returned when you returned. And later I sat in shadow to sculpt silently and alone these clay tablets.

Guernica, 1983-1988

DE *EL RACIMO Y LA ESTRELLA* (2002)

FROM *RACEME AND STAR* (2002)

Exploracion de la Amada
(fragmentos)

1.
Sobre la mesa está el pan.
Está el pan sobre la mesa.
Nutritiva fortaleza.
Quintaesencia del afán.
Firme calor que le dan
aquí se siente y conforta.
Una harina de ala corta
se fatiga en el mantel.
Sí con sal, y no con miel,
pero es miel lo que reporta.

Ahora tu mano lo toma.
Ahora tu mano lo deja.
Tu mano, como una abeja,
como una abeja o paloma.
Y cuando tu mano asoma
baja su frente dorada,
abre su pupila armada
de una caliente ternura.
Y te mira en la espesura
de su miga compactada.

Tu mano, el otro alimento;
el pan, alimento puro:
doble contacto procuro
de esos tactos avariento.
En el pan tu mano siento
como una rosa de giro:
cómo puedo, cuando miro
tu mano, no ver al pan

THE LOVER, EXPLORED
(fragments)

1.
The bread is on the table.
On the table is the bread.
Source from which strength is fed.
Quintessence of what's desirable.
Steady and tangible,
a heat that gives comfort.
Flour, its wings short,
rests on the cloth, too tired to go.
With salt, yes, and honey, no,
but it brings honey of some sort.

Now your hand takes up the loaf.
Now your hand sets it free.
Your hand, it is like a bee,
like a bee or a like dove.
When your hand finds the trove
under its gold crust, then
its guarded eye opens
with a warmth of tenderness.
And it looks at you from the thickness
of its tightly-knit grain.

One food, your hand, nutrient-rich;
the other, the bread, pure:
a double contact I procure
when I make this hungry reach.
In the bread it's your hand I touch,
like a rose that's changed identity:
how can I not, when I see
your hand, see the bread, too,

que harinoso del afán
se levanta en un suspiro?

No se marchen de la mesa
nunca, nunca se me esfumen:
unidos son el resumen
primario de la belleza.
Todo se compendia en esa
deliciosa conjunción:
pan y mujer, sabia unión
que con mucílago puro
sostiene el deber oscuro
que gobierna al corazón.

4.
Déjame verte despacio.
Ahora quiero ser moroso.
Entrar en tu cuerpo hermoso
es como entrar en palacio.
Ondulación de topacio,
festejo de curvatura.
Cómo crece tu estatura.
Cómo crece y se completa.
En la dimensión secreta
tienes llave y cerradura.

Nave sin puntal, abierta.
Ojiva de noche y astro.
Huella de mi pulso. Rastro
de mi pisada más cierta.
Mano en alto, luz alerta,
hacia tu abismo me lleno
mientras sucedo sereno
entre los pozos del mundo.
Yendo adelante, me hundo
para erigirme más pleno.

the flour of all I'm eager to do
rising in a single sigh.

At this table they never leave me,
they never simply disappear.
When they are together here,
they are the sum of all beauty.
In that delicious unity,
everything is compounded:
wise union, woman and bread,
which, with a pure viscosity,
nourishes that obscure duty
by which the heart is led.

4.
I want to slacken the pace.
Let me look at you slowly.
To enter your beautiful body
is like going into a palace.
A topaz, undulating grace,
you are curving's feast-day.
How your presence holds sway,
how it grows, and grows complete.
In the realms of what's secret
you're the key and the locked-away.

Nave without supports, open.
Arch made of stars and nightfalls.
You are the footprints of my pulse,
of all my traces, the most certain.
My hand raised, the light awakened,
you are the chasm with which I am filled
while I carry on, peaceful,
though I tread near the well's edge.
In my going forward I submerge
myself, to rise even fuller still.

Eres nocturna y luciente:
eres como campo arado:
dos brasa te han germinado
oscuras bajo la frente.
Caminando febrilmente
voy por tierra de aradura,
y en la hojarasca madura
que tu espacio fertiliza
siento en mi avance la brisa
feraz de la agricultura.

Órbita de la distancia.
Amplitud de la extensión.
Para andarte el corazón
no me basta sólo el ansia.
Inteligencia, ignorancia,
lucidez, sueño, olvido.
Todo el aire se ha extendido
con música, galopante,
y yo voy de caminante
con el pulso estremecido.

9.
Me gusta verte ladear
sobre el hombro la cabeza.
Casi la oreja te besa—
caracola de la mar—
el hombro suave al bajar.
Como guajaca dormida
se despierta retenida,
al bajar, tu cabellera.
Y tu mano volandera
ya la tiene sostenida.

Un ademán, siendo tuyo,
es como rosa cifrada.

You are the brilliance and the night:
you are a field of new furrows:
darkly, underneath your brows,
two coals grow the seeds of light.
I go as a fevered man might,
through earth given to the plow,
where ripened, fallen leaves now
feed your space with fertilities,
and I face into the fruitful breeze
of the croplands as I go.

Orbit of all that's far off.
That stretch, how full and apart.
In order to reach your heart
longing is not enough.
Intelligence, what's dreamed of,
ignorance, forgetting, lightfalls.
All the air is nothing else
but music set to a gallop,
and I go step after step
with my trembling pulse.

9.
I like it when you lean
your head to your shoulder until
your ear, that sea shell,
comes near the smooth shoulder bone,
nearly kisses it, lowering down.
Like the limbs of the guajaca
tree, falling yet held back,
when you lean your head your hair
hangs asleep in mid-air,
till your hand plays it awake.

A gesture, being yours,
is like a rose in code.

Circularidad radiada.
Universo en un capullo.
Movimiento menor—cuyo
soplo gira al infinito—
es en ti cóncavo grito,
hipérbole de voz plena:
cada gesto tuyo llena,
deja al horizonte ahíto.

Eres del espacio dueña
y dueña del movimiento.
Dentro del giro del viento
oscilas como una enseña.
Muda danza te diseña
con dibujo imperceptible.
Tu arquitectura es flexible
como un círculo movido.
Estás llena de sonido.
Tu movimiento es audible.

Ahora vive. Gira. Anda.
Vuelve. Salta. Sube. Inclina.
Dobla la cintura fina.
Baja como una alamanda.
Asómate a la baranda
de la vida, como un río
de gracia, en el poderío
undoso de tu fulgor.
Libertad. Cárcel de amor.
En ti preso, a ti me fío.

13.
Te agigantas como un río
desbordado de mis manos.
Tus perímetros livianos
tienen su propio albedrío.

Circularity radiated.
A bud that holds the universe.
A motion—whose breath stirs
the turning infinitude—
is in you a concave howl,
hyperbole, full-throated:
each act leaves something full,
leaves the horizon sated.

The owner of space, the queen,
proprietress of all motions.
Wherever the wind spins
you waver like an ensign.
Silent, the shape you dance in,
an outline that's imperceptible.
Your architecture's as flexible
as a circle that moves and bends.
You are full of sounds,
you are motion made audible.

Now live, and turn, and stroll.
Return. Leap. Climb. Lean.
Bend, at your slender waist, down
to the low growth, that small.
Stretch yourself to the rail
of your life, a river of grace,
the strength of your brilliance
in wave upon wave.
Liberty. Prison of love.
Captive in you, my deliverance.

13.
Overflowing my two hands,
you rise like a river's
crested, shifting perimeters,
answering to your own demands.

A tu cintura confío
el poder de la angostura.
Aro de tu arquitectura
que se reduce, contrario.
Lo otro—multitudinario—
va creciendo en la espesura.

Tu cabello es aluvión
que ensombrece la mirada.
Tu labio es fruta cortada
que acaricia la extensión.
Tu seno es la difracción
más opulenta y frutal.
Tu vientre es equinoccial,
mas de toda latitud.
Y cuando bajo el talud
el crecimiento es total.

Cómo caben en tu falda
tus arquitrabes redondos?
Tus omóplatos—orondos
y breves—van por tu espalda.
Tus dedos, como guirnalda
viva, se afilan y trenzan.
Tus atributos se inmensan
entre los brazos que tiendo.
Tu cuerpo es como un estruendo.
Todas tus porciones piensan.

En qué exacta proporción
y con qué medida justa
tu cuerpo se desajusta,
que crece sin remisión?
Con estas manos que son
manos porque en ti se hallan,

To your waist I commend
all the powers of narrowness.
Your architecture's circumference
that grows contrary, lessens.
The rest, in its abundance,
fills the thickets with excess.

A dark alluvium, your hair,
that shadows your face.
Your lips, a fruit that's been sliced,
caressing everywhere.
Your breast is a fruit-bearing,
opulent diffraction.
Your belly is a collection
of all latitudes, equinoctial.
And where I descend the hill,
all is increase and addition.

The architraves of your hips,
how does your skirt hold them?
Your shoulder blades, small domes
where your back slopes.
Like a live wreath your fingertips
taper and interlink.
All your attributes burgeoning
in these arms that hold you.
Your body's a clamor, a row.
All your portions think.

In what exact proportion
and with what precise gauge
does your body disarrange
itself to increase without end?
These hands, which find they are hands
by finding themselves in you first,

porque en torno de ti estallan
con la fiebre de la vida,
puedo darte la medida
que tus porciones ensayan.

and which, around you, burst
with living's fever,
can provide you with the measure
that your parts put to the test.

DE *PASANDO POR UN TRILLO* (1997)

From *Along the Trail* (1997)

TORO

Por un trillo mágico
el toro Crisóstomo.
Qué toro más gordo,
qué toro tan pálido.
Qué toro más torvo,
qué toro tan ácido.
Qué toro más plomo,
qué toro tan fláccido.
Qué toro más sordo,
qué toro tan drástico.
Qué toro más bobo,
qué toro tan cáustico.
El toro Crisóstomo
por un trillo mágico.

Bull

Along the magic trail
comes the bull Crisóstomo.
What bull more fat,
what bull so pale.
What bull more grim,
what bull so sour.
What bull more leaden,
what bull so flabby.
What bull more deaf,
what bull so drastic.
What bull more stupid,
what bull so caustic.
The bull Crisóstomo,
along the magic trail.

TESORO

Una tinaja insólita
es ésta, amigo,
que yace en un rincón
de mi recinto:
el agua de su vientre
se le ha perdido
y esconde avariciosa
y con cariño
un fragmento de cielo
y un rayo fijo,
una almendra pulida
y un albo río,
un cocuyo andariego
y un lento grillo,
una insignia de fuego
en un camino,
una espuela de plata
con un estribo
y un machete afilado
de tiempo antiguo.
Si la vuelco de golpe
todo, mi amigo,
se escapará volando
al llano mío
y encontrará de súbito
su exacto sitio.

Treasure

An extraordinary jar
is this, friend,
that lies in the corner
of my space:
it has lost the water
in its belly
and hides greedily
and carefully
a fragment of sky
and a fixed beam,
a polished almond
and a white river,
a restless firefly
and a slow cricket,
a flag of fire
on a road,
a spur of silver
with a stirrup
and a sharpened machete
from long ago.
If I knock it over,
my friend,
it will all go flying
to my plains
and find suddenly
its precise place.

BRASA

Mi padre ha llegado
desde la laguna
sin haber pescado
biajaca ninguna.

    Madre, cómo brilla
    la brasa en la hornilla.

Mi padre ha llegado
de manigua espesa
sin haber cazado
ni un sola pieza.

    Madre, cómo brilla
    la brasa en la hornilla.

Yo no quiero caza
ni pesca yo quiero:
quiero ver la brasa
viva en el brasero.

    Madre, cómo brilla
    la brasa en la hornilla.

GLOWING COAL

My father is back tonight
from fishing the lagoon
where not one fish would bite
all the afternoon.

> Mother, the coal is so bright
> in the little stove tonight.

My father is back tonight
from thickets he was hunting
but no game came in sight
and he didn't shoot one thing.

> Mother, the coal is so bright
> in the little stove tonight.

I don't really want game,
and more than fish I love
to stare at the living flame
of the coal inside the stove.

> Mother, the coal is so bright
> in the little stove tonight.

LECCIÓN

En escuela de yerbas
aprendo de verdad.
Ellas crecen y crecen
y crecen sin cesar
con verde crecimiento
que no sabe final.
Si les dejan la tierra
toda la cubrirán
cerrando superficies
de oscuro mineral,
de tierra desgranada
o imposible de arar.
Con nombres diferentes
y semejante afán
llevan pisada firme,
silenciosa y tenaz
y siendo tan pequeñas
gritan con claridad
que si vamos unidos
avanzaremos más,
hasta que el mundo todo
luzca un verde total.

LESSON

In school I'm really
learning about grasses.
They grow and they grow
and they grow continually,
a green growth
that knows no end.
Left alone they'll cover
the whole earth,
closing over dark
mineral surfaces,
over ground unseeded
or impossible to plow.
With different names
but a like hunger
their step is steady,
silent and persistent
and being so small
they shout out clearly
that if we go together
we advance farther,
until all the world
shines completely green.

QUINQUÉ

Al centro de comedor
    el quinqué
con su tranquilo fulgor.
    Quinquerere,
    quinquerí:
    ¡Ahora mismo
    lo encendí!

Con su vientre cristalino
    el quinqué
nos ilumina el camino.
    Quinquerere,
    quinquerá:
    ¿Qué no ve?
    ¡Ya verá!

Nos alumbra la saleta
    el quinqué
a la familia completa.
    Quinquerere,
    quinqueró:
    Todo el sitio
    se alumbró.

Por el cuarto mi hermanita,
    y el quinqué
entre sus puños gravita.
    Quinquerere,
    quinqueré:
    Es ya tarde:
    ¡lo apagué!

OIL LAMP

In the middle of the dining room
    the oil lamp
quietly dispels the gloom.
    Lamp-a-lay,
    lamp-a-lo:
    I lit it just
    a moment ago.

With its belly of shiny glass
    the oil lamp
lights the way on which we pass.
    Lamp-a-lay,
    lamp-a-loo:
    You can't see now?
    Well, you're going to.

It fills the little room with light
    the oil lamp
where all the family is met tonight.
    Lamp-a-lay,
    lamp-a-lo:
    The whole place
    is all aglow.

Off to bed goes my little sis,
    and the oil lamp
rests between her two fists.
    Lamp-a-lay,
    lamp-a-lie:
    It's already late:
    flame, goodbye!

Pozo

Al romper el alba
cálida de agosto
los niños subimos
a mirar el pozo.
Qué tamaño tiene.
Qué lejos el fondo.
Al brocal pegados
unimos los hombros.
Orillas de piedras
bajan en redondo
vestidas de musgo
húmedo y verdoso.
El agua descansa
hundida en lo sólido
con profundo peso,
frío y misterioso.
Tendida debajo
nos mira a nosotros
con rápidos visos
y gráciles ojos.
Nosotros miramos
con cara de asombro.
Callados estamos,
pegando los rostros.

WELL

At break of day
in hot August,
we children climb
to look at the well.
How big it is.
How far it goes.
Shoulder to shoulder
we stand at the rim.
The stone edge
descends in a circle
clothed in moss
greenish and damp.
The water rests
its sunken weight
deep on the rock-bottom,
cold and mysterious.
Spread out below
it shows us ourselves
in quick glintings
and with delicate eyes.
We are looking
with astonished faces.
We are silent,
cheek beside cheek.

DE *TABLILLAS DE BARRO* (1996)

FROM *CLAY TABLETS* (1996)

PONIENDOME EN PIE, juro: Aquí están las raíces.
En el desarticulado volante de los relojes, están las raíces.
Antes que la corola convoque al insecto, están las raíces.
En los pelos del hocico del gato inmóvil, están las raíces.
En la parábola trémula y exacta de tus caderas, están las raíces.
En el rizo vacío del último discurso, están las raíces.
En el paso febril de Ponce de León, están las raíces.

Advierto que están en tus ojos, oh Nefertiti.
Has de saber que están aquí, oh Diógenes.
Gregorio de Nacianzo, en esto que fluye hacia la muerte.
En esto que se elonga y estalla, hermano Einstein.
Abuelo Darwin, en esto que se escoge brutalmente.
Están estando en una terrible estadía.
Reviviendo en un vivo desvivir.

Están acaso en el húmero? Sí, pero en el fémur.
Están acaso en la válvula? Sí, pero en el grifo.
Acaso en el considerando? Sí, pero en el dictamen.
Acaso descienden aquella colina enrojecida de agosto?
Sí, cómo no, por aquella lámina de homérica espuma.
No hablo de otra cosa que de las raíces. Es de las raíces,
oh tú, buen redactor, Vivaldi. Lo juro, poniéndome de pie.

RISING TO MY FEET, I swear: Here are the roots.
In the dismantled flywheel of the clocks, the roots.
Before the dawn summons the insects, the roots.
In the whiskers of the still cat, the roots.
In the tremulous, precise parabola of your hips, the roots.
In the vacant ringlet of the latest speech, the roots.
In the fevered passage of Ponce de Leon, the roots.

I say that they lurk in your eyes, oh Nefertiti.
You know that they're here, oh Diogenes.
And Gregorio de Nacianzo, in what flows toward death.
In what stretches and bursts, brother Einstein.
Grandfather Darwin, in what is selected brutally.
Terrible, their stay here.
Reviving in a vivid craving.

Perhaps they're in the humerus? Yes, and in the femur.
Perhaps they're in the valve? Yes, and in the spigot.
Perhaps in the pondering? Yes, and in the decision.
Perhaps they descend that reddened hill of August?
Of course, through that sheet of Homeric foam.
I speak of nothing but roots. It's about roots,
Vivaldi, you competent stylist. I swear it, rising to my feet.

Un poquito más de desorden, sembrador.
Piensa en la calabaza, a quién quiere de vecina?
Se volvió cartesiano el vuelo de la abeja.
Abejea un poco más, abeja. Moscardonea otro tanto,
moscardón. Zarcillo a regla, cómo es posible?
Cada fruto en su estrato, en sus penínsulas de sombra,
bajo sus continentes de luz, sobre sus socavones y cúmulos.

Creación, tan urgida de caos!

Un caos, creación considerada, que suelta y embrida.
Una disciplina móvil, remontada de horizontes.
Aquí el faisán, libre, cautivo de espesura.
Lindes. Pero lindes libres.
Entrando y saliendo, en la radiada superficie.

Voy a poner ahora la mano en tu corazón.
Oh matemática de expansión y compañía.
Tolerada simetría, cuya perfección abruma,
como función no criada por criatura.
Sin embargo, los brazos. Pero exactos?
Redimido equilibrio que se sujeta zafándose.
Empero el orden es bonito: agradable a los ojos.
Jardín inglés, qué nave varada en la acompasada espuma.
Pero afuera, en lo verdaderamente cierto,
cada parte es absolutamente propia, siendo la parte!
Un poquito más de desorden, sembrador.
Toda creación es un caos que se organiza de continuo.

A LITTLE MORE DISORDER, seed-sower.
Think of the calabash, who does it want for neighbors?
The flight of the bee turns Cartesian.
Bee a little more, bee. Double your bluebottling,
bluebottle. Rulered vine, how is it possible?
Each fruit in its stratum, its peninsulas of shadow,
under its continents of light, on its tunnels and heapings.

Creation, so urged out of chaos!

A chaos, creation pondered, that sets loose and reins in.
Discipline in motion, flown horizons.
Here is the pheasant, free, captive of thickets.
Borders, but free borders.
Coming and going, the radiated surface.

Now I'm going to touch my hand to your heart.
Oh math of expansion and togetherness.
Tolerated symmetry, whose perfection overwhelms,
the way nothing reared by any being does.
And still, the arms. But exactly?
Redeemed balance subjected in its escape.
And yet order is lovely: easy on the eyes.
English garden, beached boat in the rhythmic foam.
But outside, in the truly certain,
each part is absolutely right, being the part.
A little more disorder, seed-sower.
All creation is a chaos constantly shaped.

YO RECONOZCO UN SITIO BUENO para morir
que es donde se ha vivido viviendo.
Entonces oigo una voz: Por qué te apegas, Segismundo?
Vas y vienes, de polvo, nonato y póstumo.
Embotellado en órbitas polvorientas.
Pero yo sé que el universo estalla desde un punto:
tan reducido y denso, que todo lo contiene.
Abertura radiada e infinita
desde aquella nuez no escogida, pero ya escogida.
Estás siempre potente, pero no patente.
O bien patente, pero con permiso de la potencia.
Al menos hay un ánfora para catorce aceites.
Al menos, con una médula, se sorbe un hueso.
No soy aquel que suscribe con pies distantes.

Me he situado en el círculo
y disparo mis flechas girando con el suelo.
Ah tú, que estás en la otra abscisa,
la anterior y la posterior, ves los cometas de mi sangre?
Sin embargo, yo no he cantado para ti.
Esta rústica música busca otros pies próximos,
ajetreados en el polvo que a mí se me dio.
Equilibrio en el polvo la silla, con sus cuatro sostenes justos.
Leo mi página en el atril, contra el viento.

Entonces oigo la voz: Por qué te apegas, Segismundo?
Porqué sé que hay un solo sitio bueno para morir:
aquel que nos ha escogido el Todo.

I KNOW A GOOD SPOT for dying,
a place where our living's been lived.
Then I hear a voice: Why so attached, Segismundo?
You come and go, from dust, unborn and posthumous.
In the dusty bottles of the eyes.
But I know the universe explodes from a point:
so reduced and dense it contains everything.
Radiating, infinite opening
from that unchosen nut, but chosen now.
You are always potent, but not patent.
Or patent, yes, but by potency's leave.
At least there's an amphora for fourteen oils.
At least, with a marrow, the bone can be sucked.
I am not one who signs on from a distance.

I have placed myself in the circle
and I shoot my arrows that turn with the earth.
Ah you, who are on the other axis,
the before and after, do you see the comets of my blood?
Still, I have not sung for you.
This rustic music looks for nearer steps,
scuffling in the dust that is given me.
I balance my chair in the dust, with its four good supports.
I read my page on the lectern, against the wind.

Then I hear a voice: Why so attached, Segismundo?
Because I know there is one good place for dying:
that which the All has chosen for us.

ATENTO. Con los ojos adheridos.
Atento. Todas las herramientas en vilo.
Con la sangre suspendida, y expectante.
Memoria de la luz, del episodio y el verbo.

Ah, la productividad del tiempo.

Algo, protoplasmático, sucede.
Algo, secuela y síntoma. Adherencia del agua
en el borde del vaso. Aparición de hormigas.
Espirales de buitres en el blanco vacío.
Despunte de capullo. Un giro de crisálida.

No sucedió con la víspera.
No ocurrirá en lo postrimero.
Es una cantidad que colorea al cuadrante.
Unos pasos sin cuerpo que avanzan en la sombra.
Cantando en la épica del segundo.
Oscilando en la balanza del minuto.

Es algo firme, sin antenas.
Sucediendo en la integridad de la bóveda.
Sin armas ni pañuelos. Va cantando bajito,
sin despegar los labios: *Todo el día,*
y en todas partes...

Tú que te sientas a medir
y a tamizar palabras, atento, con los ojos
expectantes, y en la memoria de la luz.

ATTENTIVE. With your eyes glued.
Attentive. All the tools poised.
With the blood suspended, and expectant.
Memory of light, of event and verb.

Ah, the productivity of time.

Something, protoplasmic, happens.
Something, consequence and symptom. Water sticking
to the rim of the glass. The appearance of ants.
Circling vultures in the empty white.
Sprouting of buds. A spinning of chrysalis.

Nothing happened on the eve.
Nothing will occur in the end.
A quantity that colors the quadrant.
Bodiless steps that advance in shadow.
Singing in the epic of the second.
Oscillating in the scales of the minute.

It's something firm, without antennas.
Happening in the vault's wholeness.
Without weapons or bandanas. It sings softly,
without opening its lips: *All day,
and everywhere…*

You who sit down to measure
and sift words, attentive, with eyes
expectant, in the memory of light.

YO HE DICHO QUE CONOZCO un espacio.
Un espacio que fluye en órbitas, cúbico y velocísimo.
Con espectros brillantes, ocupados, febriles.
Con episodios altos, verdes, graduales.
Con matojos y reses, con caballos y espumas,
con maíces y postes de alumbrado.
Retículos del tiempo, y desde allí la hora
subiendo como garza hacia la redondez llameante.

Cadmo que va sembrando sus dientes,
el hombre, dentro del espacio. Aquí estoy, con mi espacio.
Hasta el fondo. Viniendo desde el fondo.
Repaso, como un escolar de Súmer,
los apretados signos. Yo mismo soy un árbol,
aquel que parte al alba, el que torna en la noche.
Escojo para mí, y sin consulta previa,
el ámbito. Uso el derecho a juntar
la vértebra y el polvo, la memoria y la voz, sangre y savia.

Con los brazos que vine, partiré. Pero me fueron dados
para la agregación continua. Y para el ejercicio
de una saturación azul, de la elaboración lenta
del anillo. Aquí estoy, con mi espacio.
Hasta el fondo. Viniendo desde el fondo.
Soy un simple soldado del menester del polvo.
Nadie me dijo: Toma, Hesíodo.
Yo mismo me situé en la fila, abriendo bien los ojos,
a la hora en que me asenté sobre mis propios huesos.

I HAVE SAID THAT I KNOW a space.
A space that flows in orbits, cubic and rushing.
With brilliant spectrums, busied, hectic.
With noble happenings, green, gradual.
With bushes and beasts, horses and foam,
with corn and lightposts.
Nets of time, and from there the hour
climbing like a heron for the blazing vault.

Cadmus sowing his teeth,
the man, in his space. I'm here, with my space.
At the bottom. Coming from the bottom.
I go over, like a Sumerian scholar,
the crowded signs. Myself, I am a tree,
that which sets out at dawn, and returns at night.
I choose for myself, without prior inquiry,
my scope. I use the right to join
vertebrae and dust, memory and voice, blood and sap.

The arms I came with, I'll go with. But they were given me
for constant addings-on. And for the exercise
of a blue saturation, of a slow elaboration
of the ring. I am here, with my space.
At the bottom. Coming from the bottom.
I am a simple soldier whose duties are dust's.
No one tells me: Take this down, Hesiod.
I placed myself in the line, eyes wide open,
the moment I sat down in my own bones.

Y BIEN ESTÁ QUE YO, que soy un pobre diablo,
me cante un salmo: Loado sea el día cuando aparece
en las jambas gastadas, cuando se va
con pañuelos oscuros por las tapias,
y sea para siempre ensalzado en los caminos,
en los recesos de los escolares, en las meriendas
de los obreros, en las curvas blancas
de las cariátides, y entre los mármoles del bosque.

Loada sea el alba cuando lee febril su partitura
y cuando el soldador baja su máscara,
en el instante mismo en que aquel gladiador de la orilla
vio nacer de su casco cuatro águilas caudales.
Loada sea cuando la niña trenza su trenza
y el pequeño varón traza el navío absorto de la noche.
Loada cuando el tímpano asordó las campanas
y la leche cerró su rostro con la nata.

Loada sea la mañana cuando partimos hacia la penuria
sin botones, sin suelas, con cucharas de ácido.
Loada sea cuando el limón fermenta al cemento
y nos satura la melancolía de la sed y del hambre.
Loada porque estamos vivos, latiendo en el espacio,
fluyendo con Heráclito hacia todos los capítulos.

Está muy bien que yo me cante un salmo, que yo sea
el arpista, el que oye, el que dice las gracias
y el deseo. Yo voy por entre el polvo,
y soy de polvo, y urdo mi destino con manos polvorientas.

IT IS WELL THAT I, a poor devil,
sing me a psalm: Praised be the day, when it appears
in the worn doorjambs, when it leaves
with its dark scarves along the walls,
and be it praised forever in the streets,
in the schoolchildren's recesses, the workers'
afternoon morsel, in the white curves
of the caryatids, among the wood's marble figures.

Praised be the dawn's hectic reading of its score
and when the welder lowers his mask,
in the very moment when that gladiator of the shore
saw four great eagles born from his helmet.
Praised be the child when she braids her braids
and the small boy draws his ship entranced by the night.
Praised when the eardrum deafened the bells,
and the milk covered its face with cream.

Praised be the morning when we set out toward poverty
without buttons, without shoe soles, with spoons of acid.
Praised be when the lemon ferments in cement
and when sorrow drenches us with hunger's thirst.
Praised because we are living, pulsing in space,
flowing with Heraclitus toward every chapter.

It is well that I sing me a psalm, that I be
the harpist, the one who hears, who tells his thanks
and desire. I go amid the dust,
and I am of dust, and I plot my destiny with dusty hands.

Venir, de abajo, como un sismo. Venir
de abajo, como una semilla. Contrayendo la tierra
y asomando la luz, donde dirime el viento.
Alzarse con las manos componiendo el destino,
oh vértebras unidas, oh Mozart invisible.

Y dónde está la vista? Tiene que estar:
ella debe urdir la tromba,
espejo de ecuaciones sucesivas,
agua dentro de agua, polea de las lontananzas.
La vista convocó a los ujieres de la sangre,
con el cetro aunador de la vista.
Hay que saber a dónde va, gritó el músculo;
gritó el concepto: A dónde se va?
A dónde, a dónde, a dónde...? Y se fueron cayendo los naipes
lilas de preguntas, pero el cuerpo anduvo,
sentado, sin andar, levantándose, entonces, para andar.

Venir, de abajo, con órbitas propias.
Y desde abajo, con las ajenas, sumadas por el brindis
de las propias. Venir con la saturación
de lo que existe, en el instante mismo
en que asomamos, sismo o planta, hacia la vida.

To COME, FROM BELOW, like an earthquake. To come
from below, like a seed. The earth contracting,
the light coming up, where the wind annuls.
To rise with hands that shape destiny,
oh joined vertebrae, oh invisible Mozart.

And where is the sight? It's necessary:
it should plot the whirlwind,
mirror of successive equations,
water within water, pulley of distances.
Sight summoned the doorkeepers of the blood,
with the unifying scepter of the eyes.
One has to know where it goes, cried the muscle;
cried the concept: Where is it gone to?
To where, to where, to where...? And the lilac cards
of questions were falling, but the body walked,
sat, not walking, got up, then, in order to walk.

To come, from below, with one's own eyes.
From below, with what is another's, added by offerings
from what is ours. To come with the saturation
of what exists, in the very instant
in which we rise up, earthquake or plant, toward life.

QUE CADA CANTOR cante a su sazón.
Que cada laúd vibre con uñas propias.
Que cada acento caiga, como un péndulo,
sobre su propia ola.
Y que el mar numeroso del sonido
asorde la extensión, como un deslinde de gaviotas.
Cada uno bien parado
sobre su sombra.

Aquellos que se acercan
con compases y finas mondaderas
que se los lleve el viento agudo de las nieblas.
Cada uno con su canto
a lo largo del áspero silencio
y sobre las sonantes aceras
y adentro de los establos
y las bodegas
y en las esquinas más comidas
de sombra al fondo de las bibliotecas.

Allí estaremos todos
en el mismo saliente de destino,
ansiosos de belleza.
Soledad del solista con que se cuaja el coro.
Oh el avatar de un pulso que pulsa la tormenta.
Allí todos, en vilo,
número y rostro,
conquistando la misma tierra,
explorando los mismos pozos,
esculpiendo en los ojos idénticas estrellas.

MAY EACH SINGER sing in his season.
May each lute be sounded by the right nails.
May each accent fall, like a pendulum,
on its own wave.
And may the seas of sound
deafen the expanse, like a stretch of seagulls.
Each one standing firm
on his shadow.

Those who approach
with compasses and garden shears,
may they be brought the keen wind of fogs.
Each with his song
through the whole harsh silence
and above the sonorous sidewalks
and inside the stables
and the shops
and in the most shadow-filled
corners in the bottoms of libraries.

There we will all be
on the same verge of destiny,
anxious for beauty.
The soloist's solitude connecting the choir.
Oh the avatar of a pulse that touches the storm.
All there, expectant,
number and face,
winning the same ground,
exploring the same dusts,
sculpting identical stars in our eyes.

Yo TRANSITO LAS PIEDRAS que transito
con la propagación del que sucede
de voz a canto, de silencio a grito.
Mudez acústica que junta y puede.

No me distancio del pedrusco pardo
ni me margino del esparto breve:
con los pies me cosecho en lo que ardo
y me adelanto con lo que se mueve.

En aquello que para, me detengo:
ya me encamino, si comienza a andar:
y porque me conozco en lo que vengo
sé que voy, recto, del arroyo al mar.

Aquella flor que su fragancia neta
no pudo dar, bozales de infortunio,
a mí me quita un tramo de la meta
y me mutila a mí en el plenilunio.

Todos somos guerreros polvorientos
que partimos del fondo hacia la altura
para tocar más altos firmamentos
con los pies más sujetos a la hondura.

Aquí estamos, en faja de combate,
sosteniendo la lumbre lidiadora:
pronto!, no dejes que la sombra trate
de comernos, por pétalos, la aurora.

I WALK THESE STONES that I walk along
in the slow spreading of what happens
from silence to cry, voice to song.
Able and mute music that joins.

From these rocks, I'm at no remove,
from this grass, I keep no distance:
I grow myself in what I love;
with whatever moves, I advance.

In that which stops, I stop, too.
I walk when it walks, stride for stride:
and since I know myself in what I come to
I know that I go straight from stream to tide.

That flower that couldn't give its full
fragrance, muzzled by misfortune,
takes from me a piece of the goal,
cripples me under the full moon.

We are all in dust's regiments
and leave the bottom for the heights
to touch the utmost firmaments
though the depths keep hold of our feet.

Here we are, in our battle row,
helping the fighter's fire burn on:
quickly!, don't allow the shadow
to consume, through petals, our dawn.

DONDE ESTUVO AQUEL ÁRBOL de mi infancia,
uniéndome a los que deben morir antes que yo,
a los que han muerto ya,
apretando a mis hijos contra mi cuerpo,
miramos hacia abajo.

Con cinco plomos, con catorce raíles,
con veinte yacimientos de basalto,
con grúas ya compactas de angustia y esperanza.
Puse aquel peso de mis ojos en las miradas de mis hijos.
Halando con la sangre de mi estirpe.
Todos, en un anillo lleno de hélices,
donde estuvo aquel árbol de mi infancia, recuerdas?

Nos pusimos al borde del ausente;
yo, mordiendo palabras por dentro,
clamando con los fuelles bárbaros del sentido,
y todos demandamos sin separar los labios,
sumergiendo los ojos:
Sal! Vuelve! Así gritamos. Así, en medio del viento.
Así cosimos nuestros codos.
Así ceñí a mis hijos, como yemas, en torno mío.
Sal! Vuelve! Encima ardía el sol, árido como una moneda.
Sobre la frente de mis padres, mermaban sus frutos.
Sobre mi frente se fueron degradando.
Ya, encima de mis hijos, el aire era un embudo de silencio.

Esto pasó en el sitio de mi infancia
donde crecía el árbol enorme como un astillero,
que sabía venir cada año como un cuenco de dulzura,
que cargaba los pájaros como un patriarca.
Miramos hacia abajo con tendones de angustia: Sal!
Vuelve! Y lo vimos, abrirse como un arca, en la llanura.

WHERE WAS THAT TREE from my childhood,
joining me to those who will die before me,
to those who have already died,
clasping my children to my body,
we look down.

With five plumb lines, with fourteen rails,
with twenty deposits of basalt,
with cranes already filled with anguish and hope.
I put that weight of my eyes in the looks of my children.
Seeking with the blood of my lineage.
Everybody, in a ring of helixes,
where was that tree from childhood, do you remember?

We stood at the edge of the absent;
I, gnawing words inside,
clamoring with the crude bellows of sense,
and all of us demanding, without moving our lips,
immersing our eyes:
Go! Come back! Shouting thus. Thus, in mid-wind.
Thus we linked elbows.
Thus I gathered my children, like buds, around me.
Go! Come back! The sun was burning above, burning like a coin.
Over the brow of my parents, its fruits were dwindling.
Over my brow, they decayed.
Already, above my children, the air was a funnel of silence.

This happened in the place of my childhood
where the tree was growing huge as a shipyard,
that knew how to appear each year like a bowl of sweetness,
that carried the birds like a patriarch.
We're looking down with tendons straining: Go!
Come back! And we saw it, opening like an ark on the plain.

Hacia arriba! Adentro de la muerte está la vida.
El húmedo carbón se enciende con la fricción de la sangre.
Palissy que no ceja, la sangre combustiona las estrellas.
A través de la sangre se captan los mejores
horizontes. Son valles ondulantes y de oro, y en los linderos
azules altas torres se alzan para medir las distancias.

Para alcanzar lo hondo, tener los ojos altos.
Para alcanzar lo alto, tener los pies hundidos.
Adentro de la muerte está la vida.
La muerte es la estación más frutecida y roja.
La muerte es el portillo, el alféizar, la larga pértiga.
En los bolsillos de la muerte pululan las almendras infinitas.

He aquí que no hablo de esa corona trémula,
de ese paso convulso que derrama hacia el mundo
el fuego que alentaba en sólo un vaso.
Hablo de las secuencias diarias, de los fragmentos
y polvillos lentos, del más continuo
ejercicio del aire dentro de su taller explosivo.
Del alma costillada como un arca
con la creación dentro, salvando los latidos más aptos.

Tú eres Noé, contigo amanecerá el día.
En ti, hoy, ahora mismo, se dirimen asuntos implacables.
No lo sabes? Tú eres el héroe, y en ti se espera.
Precisamente porque piensas que no eres el héroe, eres el héroe.
Aquellos que pasaron bajo el arco de júbilo, tú los pasaste.
Pero yo tengo las miradas bien puestas, y te digo
que el que pasaba, en verdad, eras tú.

                                    La Guérnica, 1993

UPWARD! Within death there is life.
The damp carbon is lit with the friction of the blood.
Unflinching Palissy, the blood combusts the stars.
The best horizons are had through the blood.
They are undulant valleys of gold, and on the blue
borders tall towers rise to measure the distances.

To reach the depths, raise the eyes high.
To reach the heights, keep the feet sunk in.
Within death there is life.
Death is the season most fruited and red.
Death is the opening, the embrasure, the long pole.
In death's pockets swarm the infinite almonds.

I do not speak here of that tremulous crown,
of that convulsed passage that spills toward the earth
the fire that burns in only one glass.
I speak of the daily sequences, of the fragments
and slow siftings of dust, of the constant
exercise of the air in its explosive workshop.
Of the soul ribbed like an ark
with the creation inside, saving the most apt pulses.

You are Noah, with you the day will dawn.
In you, today, even now, implacable points are dissolved.
You don't know it? You are the hero, he's looked for in you.
Precisely because you think you aren't, you are the hero.
Those who passed under the triumphal arch, you led them.
But I am attending well, and I tell you
that the one going through, in truth, was you.

Guernica, 1993

171

DE *TABLILLAS DE BARRO II* (2000)

From *Clay Tablets II* (2000)

ESTA ES LA LARGA HILERA de la noche, sobre las breves
colinas, con el polvo subiendo de los pasos.
Mirad, en la honda noche, la larga hilera
pisando las colinas polvorientas.
Mirad las negras columnas avanzando con hachas
de madera, con voces que se levantan
hacia el cielo, sonando en el parche infinito de la tierra.

Esta es la larga hilera avanzando en la noche
con la aurora en los ojos, penetrando en la niebla ensordecida.
Así pasan las voces, como frutos, de mano en mano;
así cruzan los himnos silenciosos, como agujas, cosiendo
los costillares móviles; así pisan los pies, como piedras,
las fluyentes raíces de la noche.
Esta es la euforia lenta, la lenta travesía,
la andadura remota, la remota impulsión!

Adelante, en algún sitio que está delante, fosforecen
los frutos dentro del espeso valle, fosforecen
las aguas con sus peces, fosforecen
las gloriosas panículas de junio, fosforecen
las rosas, los poemas, los panes, las medallas...
Adelante, en algún sitio que está delante, adelante!

Adelante! Ya sobreviene el día, ya vendrá el día;
he aquí el día, ya viene, ya vendrá dorando el amasijo
violento que desliza sus poleas;
oh la larga columna de seres que caminan en la noche,
la vasta hilera, sobre las inmensas colinas,
debajo de las nubes dinámicas del polvo.

THIS IS THE LONG LINE of the night, over the brief
hills, with the dust rising from their footsteps.
Look, in the deep night, the long line
treading dusty hills.
Look at the dark columns advance with wood
hatchets, with voices that rise
toward the sky, sounding the earth's infinite drumskin.

This is the long line advancing in the night
with the dawn in their eyes, penetrating the deaf mist.
Thus the voices pass, like fruit, from hand to hand;
thus they cross the silent hymns, like needles, sewing
the mobile ribs; thus the feet tread, like stones,
on the flowing roots of the night.
This is the slow euphoria, the slow crossing,
the distant progress, the distant impulsion!

Onward, somewhere up ahead, the fruits
glow in the dense valley, the waters
glow with their fish, the glorious flowerings of June
glow, and the roses, poems, breads, medallions...
Onward, somewhere up ahead, onward!

Onward! Now the day happens, now the day will come;
it is here, it is coming, it will come and gild
the turbulent mixture that spins its pulleys;
oh the long human column walking the night,
the vast line, crossing huge hills,
under dynamic clouds of dust.

Y ME GUSTÓ LA VIDA TANTO que quise, como todos,
quedarme para siempre. Oh la férvida luz,
los ojos ofrecidos de la mujer que amo...
Oh las imágenes vividas. Las vívidas imágenes
por vivir. Las miríadas de gérmenes
musicando sus himnos, las altas voluciones del azul...

Si por mí fuera, viviría siglos. Me quedaría
yendo y viniendo, tratando de entender, juntando
materias, aprendiendo oficios, proyectando y cumpliendo!
Iría de ojo en ojo de mujer, de hijo en hijo
hasta que fuese un tronco florecido
o una estatua de espuma andando contra el viento.
Cómo podría hartarme si nací para estar atento,
para meter las manos en los jergones del olvido?

Aquí estoy, con mi copa, en medio del bullicio,
cantando con los soplos memoriosos de la sangre:
Vednos aquí, de pie, alrededor de nuestros pobre huesos.
Vednos en músculos, atisbando con fúlgidas retinas.
Vednos, pulsátiles, rodando con las ruedas del amor.
Visiones dulces del que existe en medio de la luz,
con la luz en los puños, bien plantado en el vórtice!

...Epifanía de la sangre, con qué pífanos locos
se podría cantar esta totalidad jubilosa?
Qué músicos fantásticos detendrían lo que atardece?
Porque siempre atardece, siempre llega la tarde
con sus yeguas oscuras a pastar la yerba muda del corazón,
y entonces en los dientes del recuerdo
se comienza a rumiar la luz como un pan verde!

AND LIVING PLEASED ME SO MUCH that I wanted, like everyone,
to stay forever. Oh the fervid light,
the offered eyes of the woman I love...
Oh the lived images. The images, vivid
with living. The myriad seeds
musicking their hymns, the high and spinning blue...

If it were mine to decide, I'd live centuries. I'd keep
coming and going, trying to understand, combining
substances, learning trades, planning and completing!
The woman's eyes, one at a time, then child by child
until it became a tree in flower
or a statue of sea-froth going into the wind.
How could I tire of it, born to be vigilant,
to reach my hands into the bags of forgotten.

Here I am, with my glass, surrounded by noise,
singing with the long-remembering breaths of the blood:
Look at us, standing here, gathered round our poor bones.
Look at us, muscled, retinas glinting with what we glimpse.
Look at us, pulsing, turning with the wheels of love.
Sweet visions of what exists in the midst of light,
with the light in our fists, planted firm in the vortex.

...Epiphany of the blood, with what wild fifes
could this jubilant whole be sung?
What undreamt-of musics could hold off the darkness?
Because the dark falls always, the evening always arrives
with its dark mares to graze the heart's mute grasses,
and then in the teeth of memory
the light starts to get eaten away like a green bread!

MUDO ME SIENTO sobre mi propio hueso. Mudo me siento
a repasar sencillo con dientes, con tendones,
con vasos, con bolsillos, con uñas, con cordones.
Me siento a caminar por las terrazas de mi pensamiento.

Porque yo soy, y existo, y tengo ganas, cantos,
sueños, silencios, bullicios, frustraciones,
urgencias, menesteres, esplendores, quebrantos.
Tengo derecho a cantarme de punta
a punta, entrando solo a mis propias canciones.
Yo solo, en lo que soy, con mi única pregunta.

Vivo estoy, yendo y dando, juntando, siendo un siendo
que ha sido para ser, con mis sumas y restas:
igual que una explosión, vivo mi propio estruendo;
dentro de mi pregunta, me traigo las respuestas.

Oh Magnus, piensa en mí, en este de aquí ahora.
Ya no volveré a ser. Es mi única ocasión.
Yo tengo la estatura rápida de la aurora
y un nombre sobre el rojo salto del corazón.
Vibro entre dos puntos de anónima extensión
sumergido en el sueño más inquietante de la hora.

Solo me siento sobre mi propia vértebra. Solo me siento
a repasar legítimo, primario, la cifra que yo soy
con pelo, con moneda, con azufre y condimento.
Siento que la canción pasa por donde voy.
Siento que la canción se nutre vorazmente de mi aliento.

Silent, I sit over my own bones. Silent, I sit down
for a simple once-over with teeth, tendons, my own
glasses, pockets, fingernails, string.
I sit to walk the terraces of my thinking.

Because I am, and I exist, and have hankerings, songs,
dreams, silences, commotions, frustrations,
urgencies, duties, afflictions, splendors.
From one end to the other I get to sing
myself, alone, into my own song I enter,
alone with what I am, with my one question.

I live, giving and moving, joining, being a being
that has been in order to be, with my sum and difference:
like an explosion, I live my own bursting;
inside my question, I bring the response.

O Magnus, think of me here, now; I won't come
back into being. It's my one time.
I'm that quick bit of grandeur at the start
of day, a name over the red leap of the heart.
Between two points of anonymous space, I quiver,
sunk in the unsettling dream of the hour.

I sit alone, over my own vertebrae. Alone, I sit
for a genuine, fundamental review of this cipher
I am, with hair, with coins, with sulfur and savor.
I can tell the song passes through where I'm at.
I can tell that the song has my breath to devour.

VOY SIEMPRE ANDANDO,
andando, andando voy: por un largo camino
me veo partir solo, yéndome acompañado,
despidiéndome solo del tumultuoso sitio.

Sobre silencios duros,
sobre bullicios locos de hojalata expandida
equidisto los ojos celestes de mi burro,
sostengo las fanegas que cargo en mis costillas.

Yo siempre supe, siempre
tuve a bien la región vasta del nacimiento,
y me fui andando solo sobre ciscos calientes,
escribiendo en la tierra con tizne de los dedos.

Yo, vástago de yerba,
yerba yo mismo, yerba bajo el polvo irradiante
cantando con los hilos azules de la tierra
y un álgebra sutil de oscuros manantiales.

A veces me detengo
a contar rizomas como quien repasa oro,
o a deslindar las luces más altas del reflejo
o a cubicar espacios con teodolito y plomo.

Oh memorial del cielo,
cuánto cristal escrito mientras la sangre andaba:
qué de voces cantando a la luz del espejo,
qué de pulsos tranquilos sosteniendo las lámparas.

Voy siempre andando,
andando, andando voy: por un largo camino
me veo partir solo, yéndome acompañado,
despidiéndome solo del tumultuoso sitio.

Always I go walking,
walking, walking I go: down a long road
I see myself set out alone, leaving accompanied,
saying farewell, alone, to the tumult.

Over strict silences,
over the crazy clatter of tin roofs
I distance the starry eyes of my burro,
I carry the bushels of grain on my shoulder.

And always I knew, always
my thoughts turned to the vast lands of my birth,
and I went walking over warm coaldust,
writing the earth with soot from my fingers.

I, descendent of grass,
grass myself, grass under radiant dust
singing there with the blue threads of the earth
and a subtle algebra of dark springs.

Sometimes I will stop
to count rootstalks like someone who's found gold,
or to mark out the reflection's best lights,
or square-off spaces with theodolite and lead.

Oh memorial of sky,
so much written crystal while the blood walked:
all the voices singing in mirror-light,
the tranquil pulses holding up the lamps.

Always I go walking,
walking, walking I go: down a long road
I see myself set out alone, leaving accompanied,
saying farewell, alone, to the tumult.

Entonces me acordé de cuando ella cogía
ciruelas. Era agosto, y una arboleda umbría.
El mundo se iniciaba, y entre los dos corría
una tromba de amor de terrestre energía.

Era una arboleda de otro tiempo. Sentía
que, al entrar a la sombra, se entraba en una vía
de gozo, y el fulgor del rayo desleía
en el coloide verde cristales de ardentía.

Ella se adelantaba con falda tenue que exhibía
la impronta de sus muslos de suave simetría,
y cuando se inclinaba su ademán escogía
la amarillez jugosa que agosto le ofrecía.

Los remotos ciruelos abandonaban a porfía,
como viejos carteros, recados de ambrosía.
Era un suelo de hojas que al pisarse escribía
sacramentos sonoros de la ancha tierra mía.

Adentro de mi pecho—punta de la osadía,
cofre de la ventura!—la antigua letanía
igual que un epinicio agreste o ruda epifanía,
me sincopaba el verso como luz que caía.

A veces, en su escote breve, se estremecía
toda la redondez del mundo en firme algarabía,
y la audición de mis dos manos dos sirenas oía
como quien tocar quiere las mejillas del día.

Sacerdotisa del amor joven me parecía,
cuando yo era el flechero que en las hojas seguía—
ávido de memoria, de canto, de amor, de poesía—
el fulgor de su cuerpo que en la sombra fluía.

SHE WAS PICKING PLUMS; it all comes back to me.
It was August, and the grove was shady.
The world was beginning, and between her and me
rushed a whirlwind of love and earthly energy.

It was a grove from another time. It seemed to me
that the way into the shade was the entry
into delight, and the bright ray grew watery
in the green colloid crystals of love's urgency.

She went on in a thin skirt on which one could see
the imprint of her muscles, their smooth symmetry,
and when she leaned she chose from the tree
an offering of August's, a yellowness, juicy.

The far-off plums surrendered, stubbornly
as old postmen, their ambrosial delivery.
By treading the leaves I was writing a harmony
of sacraments of this wide ground, my territory.

In my chest—point of audacity,
coffer of joy—the ancient litany
like a wild epinicion or a rude epiphany,
like falling light the lines syncopated me.

At times, in her glimpsed breast, the totality
of the world's firm roundness shook unintelligibly,
and my two hands heard two sirens' melody
like one who would stroke the day's cheeks gently.

A priestess of young love she seemed to me,
and I the bowman in the leaves, pursuing avidly—
for memory, for song, for love, for poetry—
her body that flowed in the shadow brilliantly.

ME FUI A VER A MI PADRE—diciembre terminaba—
y nos sentamos en el viejo portal donde yo un día
canté copales verdes, vicarias de floral eucaristía.
Y me dijo, arropándose en sus gastadas telas,
con frase que ligaba su infancia y la mía:
desearía ver una sabana llena de aguinaldos.
Sabes cómo son esa sabanas llenas de un vestido blanco?
Padre, lo sé. También a mí, con ciertos meses,
me suben a la sangre unas olas pujantes
de ver patria pueril, primer espacio, espigas, reses!

Me fui a ver a mi padre—terminaba diciembre—
y juntos regresamos a sitios de silencio, a puntos
cuyas imágenes tan sólo pueden verse con ojos difuntos.
Y le dije, después de una pausa común
donde cada uno destrenzaba sus íntimos asuntos:
Aún quedan por aquí los enormes cocuyos
que no querían que cogiéramos, hablándonos con susto?
O cuando se agrietaba el barro del camino
aquellas mariposas que plegaban sus alas en un cúmulo?
O aquel aire tan fino que tocaba en las casas
citando con sus dedos para el convoque augusto?

Acababa diciembre. Acababa en silencio, yéndose
como un pez, fluyendo en la frialdad profunda de los cuerpos.
Mi padre se arropó en el balance mudo de la tarde
y yo partí—viajero ensimismado del recuerdo—
caminando invisible por hondos canarreos!

I WENT TO SEE MY FATHER—December was ending—
and we sat in the old porch where one day
I sang green copal trees, eucharist flowers.
And he said to me, wrapping himself in his rags,
with a line that linked his childhood and mine:
I would like to see a savannah filled with flowering.
You know, savannahs completely dressed in white?
I know, father. In me, too, in certain months,
the strong waves rise in my blood and I want
to see the country's youth, that first space, the sheaves, cattle!

I went to see my father—December was ending—
and together we went back to silent places, to spots
that can only be seen with your eyes gone.
And I said to him, after we'd both parsed
and untangled the threads of our thoughts:
Are there still those enormous fireflies here
that did't want us to catch them, speaking to us, afraid?
Or when the road mud cracked open,
those masses of butterflies folding, unfolding, their wings?
Or that fine air that touched the houses,
arranging with its fingers for the gathering of August?

December was ending. Ending in silence, going
like a fish, flowing into our bodies' bone-chill.
My father wrapped himself in evening's mute rocker
and I left—voyager sunk in his memories—
walking invisible through the deep-rutted land.

Yo saqué la guitarra bien temprano, y me puse a cantar
con la cara hacia el polvo, viendo al sol.
Aún era de mañana, y un color vangogh incineraba el pasto.
Percibí que mi voz tenía un olor a cáscara lenta.

Salí a pisar la tierra, martinferrista nuevo,
un velarde de mí, con el plectro de todos
en el bolsillo izquierdo de la camisa.
Salí a pisar la tierra, con la voz yendo de tramo a tramo.

Los que tenían trompa no me oyeron.
Oyó Jericó completa, pero mi arpa no fue escogida.
De qué tribu eres?, me increparon. No pude responder:
yo no había salido a cantar sino para una tribu anónima.

Así corrió la arena, de un vidrio a otro;
así partió cargado, y regresó cargado, el lustroso bajel.
Cuando distribuyeron los cubiertos, yo no estaba:
merodeaba allá afuera, cantando para el polvo viendo al sol.

A veces me citaron, pero me devolvían: Tiene aroma
fragoroso, es como un tubérculo, mira, Teócrito,
vuelve a tus cabras. Y en medio de un tintóreo olvido,
envuelto en tinta como un calamar, yo proseguí cantando.

Vine a quedarme, sin embargo.
Espero, como piedra, desde la altura mínima del trillo.
Porque yo canto desde temprano, como obseso,
y aún estaré cantando cuando ya sea tarde, y haya que acostarse.

Habrá que cogerme con otros dedos, pues no sirven
las bengalas, los últimos navíos, los corrillos, los pórticos.
Y yo me iré hacia aquellos que quise cantar desde siempre:
los hijos del sudor, los antiguos tubérculos del mundo!

I TOOK OUT THE GUITAR EARLY and began to sing
with my face to the dust, seeing the sun.
Morning, still, Van Gogh color burning the fields.
I could sense my voice had the smell of a slow-growing bark.

I went out to tread the earth, the new martinfiéro,
my own velarde, with the flatpick of everything
in my left shirtpocket,
I went out to tread the earth, my voice flying measure to measure.

The horn players didn't hear me.
All Jericho heard, but my harp wasn't chosen.
What tribe are you from?, they rebuked me. I couldn't answer.
I'd gone out to sing for a tribe with no name.

So the sand ran out, one glass to another;
thus it went, laden, and returned laden, the shiny vessel.
When they passed out the cutlery, I wasn't there.
I was prowling about, minstreling the dust, seeing the sun.

Sometimes they called me, but then sent me back; it smells
deafening, it's like a bulb, look, Theocritus,
go back to your goats. In the midst of a forgotten dye,
surrounded by ink like a squid, I kept singing.

I came to stay, nevertheless.
I wait like a stone from the small height of the trail.
Because I've been singing since early on, like I'm obsessed,
and I'll still be singing when it's late and I must sleep.

You will have to grasp me with other fingers, flares
are no use, nor the last ships, the cliques, the porticos.
I will go to those I wanted to sing of always,
the children of sweat, the world's ancient bulbs!

ME QUEDÉ MEDITANDO, lo incógnito en el puño:
Qué es la vida? Será una mera contracción zafada?
Será los mil semblantes de una mónada sola?
Será lo accidental que se enrumbó como una esencia?

Fui a ver la piedra para decirle: Qué es la vida?
Me senté al lado del que estaba llorando: Qué es la vida?
Del que comía por primera vez con su novia: Qué es la vida?
De Vernadski, que unía la biomasa en una cifra.
De Kandinsky, que había trazado una rayita blanca.

El que pasó vendiendo ajo puerro me dijo: Deja eso.
El administrador, de pie en la puerta: Qué te pasa?
La joven, balanceando su caderamen: No moleste.
El cirujano, de visita en casa del partero: Es tu invitado?
Yo seguí, proseguí, perseguí. Traía la pregunta
esculpida en la sangre, como el exergo bronco de una moneda.

A veces, reparando cómo se abría el clavelón, la pregunta.
A veces, viendo desfilar los trenes, la pregunta.
O viendo descender del carro al importante forastero.
O mirando las caras harinosas que exhiben los payasos.
Cómo es posible que yo tenga de por vida esta pregunta?
Cómo es posible que no pueda responderme a gusto?
Oh las tazas, las heces, el café, los labios, el sabor.
Oh la justicia, el canto, la abundancia, la paz, el éxito.
Cabello por cabello fui, indagando. Pero siempre,
manto sonoro, la cabellera general cantaba: Qué es la vida?

I STAYED MEDITATING, the unknown in my fist:
What is life? Will it be merely a crazed contraction?
Will it be the thousand semblances of a single monad?
Will it be the accidental that started out as an essence?

I went to see the stone, to say to it: What is life?
I sat alongside him who was crying: What is life?
Who was eating for the first time with his girl: What is life?
Alongside Vernadski, who was uniting the biomass with a figure.
Alongside Kandinsky, who had drawn a little white line.

One who passed by selling garlic leek said to me: Stop that.
The administrator, standing in the door: What's with you?
The young girl, swinging her big hips: Don't be a pest.
The surgeon, visiting the midwife's house: Are you invited?
I pushed on, proceeded, pursued. I brought the question
sculpted in my blood, like the rough inscriptions of a coin.

Sometimes, imitating how a marigold opens, the question.
Sometimes, seeing the trains pass by, the question.
Or seeing the important stranger descend from the car.
Or looking at the floury faces the clowns put on.
How is it possible I carry this question through life?
How is it possible I can't answer myself as I'd like?
O the cups, the dregs, the coffee, the lips, the savor.
O the justice, the song, the plenty, the peace, the success.
Hair by hair I went, ascertaining. But always,
sonorous cloak, the whole head of hair sang: What is life?

HASTA DÓNDE SOY lo que soy?
Y si lo soy, en qué medida?
Pues circunscrito siempre estoy.
Toda mi vida no es mi Vida.

Soñar del sueño que procuro.
Exploración del punto alto.
Qué me responde el aro duro?
De qué me sobro, que estoy falto?

Ah las celdillas de las horas
y los carriles que forjamos;
todas las pautas conductoras,
las finas lindes de los tramos.

Solo soy, pero no soy solo;
porque, si solo, soy un punto
que se desplaza polo a polo:
celeridad del breve asunto.

El abejar de mi conciencia,
toda la lanza de mi lanza:
voy en estado de vehemencia
desde la angustia a la esperanza.

Del sueño paso al apetito,
de la labor al rudo plato,
y estoy en grávido circuito
tocando la sangre a rebato.

Encadenado a pronta busca
de cuerpo, paso ya sin calma
en un horario que se ofusca:
sólo en futuro tengo el alma.

To what point am I what I am?
And if I'm that, in what measure?
Since I am always circumscribed.
All my living is not my Life.

To dream the dream that I look for.
Exploration of the high point.
What does the strict ring answer me?
Where the excess, and where the lack?

Ah the cells of the hive of hours
and the tracks that we are forging;
all the conductive measurings,
the lengths and their subtle boundaries.

I only am, but not alone;
because, if alone, I'm a point
that goes forth and back, pole to pole:
the quickness of this brief business.

The apiary of conscience,
all of that lance that is my lance;
with my bearing of urgency
I travel from anguish to hope.

From dream I pass to appetite,
from labor to the humble plate,
and I run the circuit burdened,
sounding the alarm of the blood.

Fettered to the body's hasty
searching, I go anxiously now
and the hours are obfuscated:
I'll have my soul in the future.

Añoro un día donde pueda,
sobre mis pies bien erigido,
dar al olvido la moneda
bajo cuya rueda me olvido.

Dejar de ser, después de todo,
este animal de loca testa
que va gastando el pobre codo
hincando al suelo su protesta.

No reducir el alma al grano
o la sustancia que incorporo:
a los demás abrir la mano
para brindar la canción de oro.

Y siento, en esta desazón,
que del ovillo del quisiera
se me va hilando la canción,
ya libre, si antes prisionera.

Advierto, si mi pecho toco,
que voy, en trueno ya seguro,
desde lo abundante a lo poco,
desde lo más claro a lo oscuro.

Júbilo grande llega a mí,
pues aprendí la lección alta:
me moriré en lo que nací,
me sobraré en lo que me falta.

Hay ciertas cúspides profundas
y ciertos géiseres morosos,
y se redimen las coyundas
con las coyundas de los gozos.

Sufrir es bueno: sufrir mucho
nos deja, como fruta al sol,

I yearn for the day I'm able,
standing square over my two feet,
to give oblivion the coin
under whose wheel I will forget.

To keep from being, after all,
this crazy-headed animal
who uses up his poor elbow
sticking his protest in the ground.

Not to shrink the soul to a speck
or to the stuff of my body:
to open the hand to others
and offer them the song of gold.

I feel, in this uneasiness,
that from the tangle of desire
is being spun for me the song,
free now, if prisoner before.

I notice, if I touch my chest,
that I go, surely, thundering
from the abundant to the scarce,
from the most clear to the obscure.

A great rejoicing comes to me,
since I have learned the high lesson:
I will die of having been born,
will exceed myself in my lack.

There are certain summits deep down,
and certain gradual geysers,
and the bindings redeem themselves
with the bindings of our delights.

To suffer is good: to suffer
much leaves us, like fruit in the sun,

al corazón perplejo y ducho:
el sufrimiento es un crisol.

En este instante considera,
por lo bruñida, ya mi frente
que lo que el pórfido macera
acaba en jugo permanente.

Todo lo acopio y sedimento,
todo lo impulso como mío:
aprendí el oficio del viento,
de las marismas, y del río!

Hasta dónde soy lo que soy?
Lo soy, en alguna medida.
Pues circunscrito y libre estoy.
Toda la Vida ya es mi vida.

in the puzzled and well versed heart:
suffering is a crucible.

In this very instant my brow,
by all that's polished, considers
that what the porphyry steeps in
ends up as a permanent juice.

All the accretions, sediments,
all the driven-ahead, like me:
I learned the office of the wind,
of the marshes and the river!

To what point am I what I am?
I'm that, in whatever measure.
Since I am circumscribed, and free.
The whole of Life is my life now.

DE *TRANSFIGURACIONES* (1999)

FROM *TRANSFIGURATIONS* (1999)

LOS SIRGADORES DEL VOLGA
(fragmentos)

Homenaje a Repin

Lo que un hombre puede ser, debe serlo.
—A. Maslow

1.
Aquí vamos halando con la fuerza
atroz de la carencia y del olvido
en voluntad enérgica y dispersa,
como un humano a bestia conducido.

Aquí vamos halando con la furia
del humillado bajo el empellón,
rellena la cabeza de la injuria
y mustio de la ofensa el corazón.

Aquí vamos halando con el lento
caminar de la grávida barcaza,
mientras aspira el corazón violento
y por los ojos la existencia pasa.

Aquí vamos halando en el sujeto
y desenvuelto pelotón de penas
desde un dinámico pulsar inquieto
que se retiene, empero, en las arenas.

Aquí vamos halando todo el peso
que suman los carriles del dolor,
inclinando los cuerpos con exceso
para que el cuerpo brinde su vigor.

THE BARGE HAULERS OF THE VOLGA
(fragments)

Homage to Repin

What a man can be, he should be.

—A. Maslow

1.
Here we are, hauling with the cruel
force of deprivation and oblivion,
with determined but unfocused will,
humans, but like beasts being driven.

Here we are, hauling with the fury
of the shoved-down, the humiliated,
heads filled with injury
and the heart, from offense, dessicated.

Here we are, hauling with the patient
steps of the barge's loaded mass,
while the heart draws its violent
breath and our eyes watch our being pass.

Here we are, in the harnessed
yet individuated troop of woes
from a pulsar, dynamic, restless,
but from these sands it never goes.

Here we are, hauling the road's sum
of griefs beneath which we stagger,
tilting our bodies into them,
the body extending its vigor.

Aquí vamos halando con los ojos
al suelo proyectados, o erigidos,
para no ver los álgidos despojos
que velan nuestros huesos preteridos.

Aquí vamos halando con la fuerte
suspensión de la sangre consumida
las espectrales cargas de la muerte
sobre las hondas aguas de la vida.

2.

Kanin, detrás del ojo con que adelante miras
late eso que ya somos desde que el dolor cubre,
como una pleura triste, nuestro ancho corazón:
tú vas viendo con dos llaves de loco espanto:
el dolor de los músculos y el dolor de los sueños:
la copa de tu angustia se recambia sus líquidos:
otros pueden volverse con un gemir tan sordo
que no se reconocen ni sus nudillos truncos,
pero tú vas poniendo cuentas como un salmista
que intercambia sonoras bandejas con los ángeles.

Aquello que se mira delante está en el fondo,
y sobre la maroma que te devana el pecho
una franja de sueño se calla destrozada:
donde mismo te quedas solo, como truncado
de una ruda ventisca que vences con la ceja,
las venas del destino se azulan y enrojecen
y se recuestan sobre su propia pesadumbre;
pero eres, sin embargo, un latido de arcilla
y pareces un lento patriarca del litoral más bajo.

Se sabe desde lejos las medallas que pierdes
y que rompes las hebras de un pórfido mayor:
se sabe que en el fondo convexo de tu frente
una torre resiste iluminando el médano:
que no puedes tener esos perros de presa

Here we are, hauling with our look
cast groundward or raised to the sky,
so as not to see the chilly dreck,
its vigil over our bones' anonymity.

Here we are, hauling with the suspended
strength of the sapped blood,
the spectral cargo of lives ended,
over the still-living's deep flood.

2.

Kanin, behind the eye with which you look ahead
is hidden that which we already are since pain covers,
like a sad membrane, our wide heart:
you see with two keys of crazed fear:
the pain of the muscles and the pain of dreams:
always a new fluid in the glass of your anguish:
others can turn away with a cry so deadened
that they don't even recognize their blunted knuckles,
but you go making litanies like a psalmist
exchanging sonorous dishes with the angels.

What's looked for up ahead is down at the bottom,
and on the tightrope that winds your chest
a fragment of crushed dream goes quiet:
right where you remain alone, as if foreshortened
by a blizzard you defeat with your brow,
your fate's veins going blue, red,
leaning over their own grief;
but you are, nevertheless, this beating clay,
like a slow patriarch of the lowest coast.

It's known from afar, the medals you lost,
and how you break the threads of a larger porphyry:
it's known that at the convex back of your forehead
a tower resists, illuminating the sands:
that you can't restrain those dogs of prey

que barren con su lengua jadeante los jardines
buscando con narices brutales la venganza:
que los barcos mejores no pasan por tu cuerpo
sino que corren dentro de tu dolor soleado!

Ves aquellas estatuas que borran sus siluetas
bajo el polvo asustado y oscuro de la muerte?
Algo viene de lejos, como estribo del fondo;
algo viene de lejos, como un gesto imposible:
abajo están los pie compactando a la duna
y una banda de fuerza eslabona los brazos.
He aquí las aspas negras del dolor cómo giran,
y advierto que atraviesa tus ojos el destino
como un águila uncida por los yugos del agua.

6.
Hala, Ilka el Marino, con músculo curvado;
mecanismo que el cuerpo distribuye e impulsa;
coyuntura que explota con el tramo vencido;
el diente contra el diente, metatarso de avance,
arco y sostén, polea de voluntad y pulso:
qué es el cuerpo? Un espacio
para halar hacia el mundo desde el mundo:
un volumen de afán en contorno flexible:
es una ergonomía sedienta
donde todo resuena, como en caja de mármol...

Ilka el Marino, hala, hala, hala!
Tira de bóvedas pedestres, de breves explosiones,
de orillas alarmadas, de cascos exprimidos:
hay que vivir, que remediar el golpe,
que cubrir con los panes las mesetas del horno:
mientrasse tengan poros, pellejos, pómulos,
ojos, pechos de obligatoria enjundia,
calcañares que tranquen como muelas
dentro de las mandíbulas estoicas del dolor.

that prowl the gardens with panting tongues,
their brutal snouts sniffing for vengeance:
that the better ships don't pass through your body
without running into your sun-bleached pain!

You see those statues that erase their silhouettes
under the frightened, dark dusts of death?
Some come from far off, like an unearthed stirrup;
some come from far off, like an impossible gesture:
their feet compact the dunes,
the taut rope links their arms.
Here are the dark braces of pain's windmill turning,
and I tell you destiny crosses your eyes
like an eagle tethered by the yoke of the water.

6.
Haul, Ilka the Mariner, with your muscles bent;
mechanism that the body pays out, impels;
joint that explodes in the vanquished space;
teeth against teeth, metatarsals advancing,
arch and support, pulley of will and force:
what is the body? A space
for hauling from the world toward the world:
a volume of energies, its contours flexible:
it's a parched ergonomics
where everything resounds, as in a marble box. . .

Ilka the Mariner, haul, haul, haul!
Pull with pedestrian vaults, quick explosions,
the alarmed shores, your soaked, crushed hooves:
you have to live, to recover from the blow,
to cover the oven rack with bread:
and meanwhile keep pores, skin, cheekbones,
eyes, the chest's necessary strength,
heels packed in like molars
in the stoic mandibles of pain.

Toda la fiera, la sustancia, el hierro,
el almidón, la fécula: todo el duro engranaje
que viene por la sangre de los días natales
y de lo prenatales: todos los eslabones
del olvido en que uno crece y donde como un móvil
echa sus sombras cuando anda:
todo cuanto es esta masa de sueño en que vivimos,
este templo veloz, esta máquina, orgánico
frontón, hacia el empuje de las sentidas cargas,
al acarreo triste, como un fleje de polvo.

Ilka el Marino, hala, hala, hala!
Cuando todo desciende y en las finas terrazas
del espíritu salta el dolor como liebre;
cuando con duro hocico el hambre baja
y muerde el pecho con diente lóbrego;
cuando por la pradera del destino
van corriendo los gamos de la suerte, veloces
como espectros, hay que tirar del cuerpo:
hay que amarrar los hombros
dentro de la humillante singladura:
hay que clavar la uña dentro del arenal caliente
para que el viento inflame las telas de los mástiles!

Every beast, substance, iron,
all the starches: all the hard cogs
turning in the blood since birth
and before; all the ties
of the forgotten in which one believes and like a mobile
throws shadows when it moves:
all is a mass of the dream we live,
this fleeting temple, this machine, organic
pediment, toward the push of feeling's freight,
the sad haulage, the bindings of dust.

Ilke the Mariner, haul, haul, haul!
When everything sifts down in the balconies
of the spirit the pain leaps like a hare:
when hunger lowers its fierce snout
and gnaws at the chest with its dark teeth;
when through the plains of destiny
the deer of good fortune come running, sped
like specters, you have to drag the body:
make a rigging of your shoulders
for the humiliating day's journey:
you have to sink your nails in the sand-heat
so that the wind ignites the raised sails.

La Voz, la Sombra, las Lanzas
(fragmentos)

III

1. Hundido en la sangre como en un vigilante batiscafo voy viendo los bosques sumergidos, los colores del silencio, el relieve oculto de las sustancias y capto declives, sorpresas, junturas, explosiones y capítulos de un libro invisible.

2. Hundido en la sangre como la punta de una sonda paso hacia las bodegas profundas del corazón, más allá de las pulseras de la alegría y toco al dolor, su nuez magullada, su manquedad de corteza, cuando ya todo es zumo dolido, sensible almendra de pudor y silencio.

3. Hundido dentro del hombre y la mujer, del anciano y del niño, del poeta y del carnicero, del desafecto y del gendarme, del joyero que se inclina sobre su lente y del chapeador que limpia los potreros. Así paso hacia el fondo con la brújula querenciosa de mi canto.

4. No puedo retenerme en los portales, así no podré ver a mi hermano en aquello que me lo hermana; no mediré con precisión el polen, no tocaré en verdad su núcleo de calor y riesgo, su lava ya vidriosa y aturdida, componencial de la especie, con sus encontronazos y truncamientos.

5. No voy a enturbiar mi canto como un agua removida por encima para que parezca profundo: yo trovo para el fondo, con la turbiedad del fondo, hacia la espiral de lo que está debajo, desde el brote verdaderamente diáfano de los manantiales submarinos.

FROM VOICE, SHADOW, LANCES
(fragments)

III

1. Sunk in the blood like a vigilant deep-sea sub, I see the under-
    water forests, the colors of silence, the dark shapes in relief, and
    I register the swales, surprises, joints, explosions, the chapters
    of an invisible book.

2. Sunk in the blood like a sounding I move toward the deep hold
    of the heart, beyond the bracelets of joy, and I touch pain, its
    bruised fruit, its damaged skin, when already everything is the
    juice of hurt, the feeling almond of shame and silence.

3. Sunk within the man and woman, the old one and the child,
    the poet and the butcher, the disaffected and the constable, the
    jeweler bent over his lens and the man who tends the pastures.
    Thus I go toward the bottom, with the longing compass of my
    song.

4. I can't stand about in the porches, or I won't be able to see my
    brother in what brothers him to me; I won't measure the pollen
    precisely, won't truly touch its nucleus of heat and hazard, its
    lava already a stunned glass, component of the species, with its
    collisions and cuttings.

5. I'm not going to muddy my song like poked-at water, just to
    make the superficial seem deep: I minstrel the depths, with the
    depths' turbulence, toward the spiral of what's underneath,
    from the truly crystalline bursts of the underwater springs.

6. Hay que bajar a los abismos como un geólogo atento y poner pequeñas banderas verdes, dejar recados de amor, adivinar torres azules allí donde gimen los descensos mayores y situarse en las encrucijadas tintóreas a repartir agua a los peregrinos, a los espesos caminantes.

7. Para qué ha de servir entonces la trabada estrofa, la destrabada antístrofa, la resonancia disparada que tiene cada secuencia eufónica? Para qué ha de servir todo este sentarse en silencio marginado un tanto del chorro de intemperie sino para irse dentro de la más abierta torrentera?

8. Hundido en la sangre como un plomo de luz o un pesado cristal o una copa que baja a recoger sombra para alzarla hacia la esmeralda hojosa de lo más alto, de lo que echa frondas y frutos hacia el sol.

IV

1. Cada auténtico canto atraviesa como un fósforo, quema las yemas del dormido: exige el coraje de la generosidad, que no espera más que cuatro onzas dentro de las nervaduras más altas.

2. Debajo del grafito y de los dedos, a partir de los resueltos labios, va creciendo como una pequeña catedral de enjundia, como una basílica de basalto y espuma noblemente dibujada y el corazón que canta es un titánico bombeo rojo, una turbina que fecunda cada surco, oh el grafito de sangre, la sangre del grafito!

3. Quién dice al cantor que cante? Todos, atravesando como un tumulto vocinglero las puertas sin sombras de su frente, bajando las copas, disponiéndose como invitados entrañables. Alrededor está el hombre sentado, como un ilustre comensal.

6. You must go down into the chasms like a watchful geologist
    and place little green flags, leave love notes, glimpse the blue
    towers there where the greater descents grieve, and place
    yourself in the tinted crossroads to give out water to the
    pilgrims, to the traveling hoards.

7. What then is the use of the well-made strophe, the antistrophe's
    un-making, that fired-off resonance that each euphonious
    sequence has? What is the use of all this sitting in alienated
    silence outdoors in the elements except to go inside the most
    open torrents?

8. Sunk in the blood like a plumb line of light or a heavy crystal
    or a cup that lowers to gather shadow and raise it toward the
    heights' leafy emerald, where fronds and fruits sprout toward
    the sun.

IV

1. Every authentic song arrives like a struck match, burns the
    buds of sleep; it demands the courage of generosity, doesn't
    expect more than four ounces of the highest ribs of the ceiling.

2. Under the lead and the fingers, from the resolute lips, it grows
    like a small, substantial cathedral, like a basilica of basalt and
    foam nobly drawn, and the heart that sings is a titanic red
    pump, a turbine that seeds each furrow, oh the lead-blood, the
    blood of the lead.

3. Who tells the singer to sing? Everyone, moving through
    doorways raucously with their unshadowed brow, lowering their
    glasses, settling in like the dearest guests. And there is the seated
    man, like a famous table-fellow.

4. Cómo medir el vino si tengo el canto, que multiplica esa rojez en las copas? Cómo voy a irme hacia mi propia médula acariciando en la soledad más sola los frutos que me ofrece la voz? Aquí están, oh hermanos, y cada canto que pongo sobre el mostrador sonoro no es sólo un viaje hacia mi pulso sino una expedición hacia los vellocinos oscuros.

5. Cada canto es un duro peligro. Entenderás tú esta gradería del espíritu hacia lo alto? Distinguirás su escala de Jacob? Percibirás las hermosas glorietas del silencio, la sinfonía salvaje de los talones que danzan en la niebla? Saludarás con simpatía a los graves argonautas que ya parten desde los versos hacia el aire, buscando lo imposible?

6. Y si viajo, Humboldt hirsuto, por tus lindes profundas extrayendo las llaves del fondo? Y si entro hacia las grandes casas, de vergonzoso bienestar, pues están rodeadas de pobreza? Y si adenso todo el dolor que no quieres oír, pues te consideras el único estratega optimista, un capitán de auroras?

7. Bajo el grafito dejo mi corazón expuesto, como un redondo ternero generoso dispuesto al sacrificio: cuídale sus grandes ojos, presérvale sus piernas nuevas, consérvale sus sonidos, que es también tu propio corazón el que brama en la luz!

VIII

1. Yo soy aquel modesto escriba que aplanó la arcilla, aguzó la madera para el rasgo, y se sentó en la hora probable de la tarde. Se podía escribir, en cuanto ya se habían iluminado las hornillas. Buscar la piedra blanca a ver qué nombre traía pues estaba confirmado el mantel de la pequeña tribu.

2. Entonces puse la tablilla sobre los muslos, y escribí palpando la tierra que me sostuvo un día desde el vientre de mi madre. Fue la tierra quien me puso contra la luz un día de espigas músicas,

4. How to measure the wine if I have the song, multiplying the red in the glasses? How to make my way to my own marrow, cherishing in the loneliest loneliness the fruits that the voice offers me? Here they are, brothers, and each song that I put on the resonant desk isn't only a traveling toward my pulse but a setting out toward the dark fleeces.

5. Each song is difficult risk. Will you know these galleries of the spirit rising toward the heights? Will you make out its Jacob's ladder? Will you perceive the beautiful bowers of silence, the wild symphony of heels that dance in the cloud? Will you greet with sympathy those worthy Argonauts departing from poems toward the air, seeking the impossible?

6. And if I travel, bearded Humboldt, through your deep boundaries extracting the keys from the bottom? And if I approach the great houses, shamefully comfortable, are they then surrounded with poverty? And if I weight all the pain that you don't want to hear, will you consider yourself the one optimistic strategist, a captain of dawns?

7. Under the lead I leave my heart exposed, like a generous, round calf set for the slaughter: take care with his big eyes, protect his new legs, save his sounds, since it's your own heart, too, that lows in the light.

VIII

1. I am that modest scribe who leveled the clay, sharpened the wood for my scripting, and sat in the likely hour of the evening. I could write, once the stoves had been lit. To search for the white stone to see what future it named and then the little tribe was sure there'd be a table to sit to.

2. Then I rested the tablet on my thighs, and I wrote, touching the earth that had sustained me since my mother's womb. The

cuando ya no se puede con las múcaras. Y yo, acordándome de todo, como el peregrino que va dando testimonio, me puse a escribir en la hora probable.

3. Evento del cual extraigo muelas de juicio, almendras de justicia, jugos de justa juglaría. A veces está dura la arcilla, y a veces es un puro juego de júbilo. A veces se junta tanto tropel de escollos para irlos salvando con prisa que el aro deja de estar cordial y cimarronea como un brinco.

4. Pero cuando ya no se puede más y rasgar el barro duele como si alguien nos escribiese con un puñal, es cuando vienen todos—mazorca amarga—a pedir audiencia. Así se me paran delante como mismo yo fui nacido, contra la luz y el viento, en un silencio de enigma y de espanto.

5. Y siento dentro del púlpito cada palabra oscura! Oigo lo que palpita por demandas en aquello que afirma y convoca cada destino, en lo que exige cada golpe eléctrico en las vértebras, lo que corre como por una atarjea musgosa de la infancia. Qué pide sino lealtad, sino sintonía, sino voluntad de canto?

6. Es tan larga la oquedad del silencio que el aliento fluye por ese túnel hasta Cánope, tan estrecho el afluente de palabras que el verbo se me zafa del labio con la rustiquez del potro; es tanta la tristeza, la pobreza tanta!

7. Así con este dolor no se eslabona, no se moldea, no se transfigura. Bajo los ojos para no ver sobre la húmeda tablilla, con el estilete en la mano; bajo los ojos para no ver, pero ya estoy viendo de memoria, dentro de la incisiva plasticidad del dolor!

earth that stood me in the light once when the grain sung, when there was no getting at the buried strata. And I, remembering everything like the wanderer giving witness, began to write in the likely hour.

3. From that event I extract wisdom teeth, almonds of justice, the juice of a just minstreling. Sometimes the clay is hard and sometimes it's a pure play of jubilation. Sometimes there gathers such a crowd of obstacles to be gotten past quickly that what would be well rounded resists and leaps away.

4. But when no more is possible and gouging the clay hurts like someone writing us with a dagger, it's when everyone comes— bitter corn—to ask an audience. Thus they appear before me as when I was born, opposed to the light and the wind, in a silence of enigma and menace.

5. And I feel inside the pulpit each obscure word! I hear the necessary throb in what affirms and gathers each destiny, in what requires each electric blow in the vertebrae, what runs as through a moss-covered drain of infancy. What does it ask but loyalty, what but wavelength, what but the will of song?

6. The cavity of silence is so wide that the breath flies through that tunnel to Canope, so narrow the flowing of words that the verb escapes from the lips with the rusticity of a colt; such is the sorrow, and so much, the poverty!

7. So with this pain there is no connection, no shape, no transfiguration. I lower my eyes so as not to see the damp clay, with the stylus in my hand; I lower my eyes so as not to see, but I am seeing from memory, in the incisive plasticity of pain!

XIII

1. Duro trasiego de ferocidades, mina de acabamientos, arena de opuestos cuerpos aproximándose. Tobillo hincado con tesón, trancada cintura, músculo constreñido para el salto con la espada, el tridente, la balanza en mano. Sólida polvareda que pasa al lobo, que desciende a la hiena, que sube al gavilán.

2. Pero arriba, al centro, dentro de la nube que acompaña al hombre como un va poroso círculo otros horizontes: tierras que adentro de sus ojos adquieren de nuevo claridad y curso, como en el prístino tiempo; que van flotando en espigas hacia la alta redondez del fruto, como una mano abierta.

3. Corros de frescura donde las manos se conocen por el tacto y las voces, saludan do y cantando cual sinsontes divinos; acequias de fulgor fluido por donde bajan los niños navegando con bordados veleros; ventanas talladas, olorosas a dulce matrimonio, en que las doncellas del espíritu estiran sus nudillos de perfume.

4. El sueño de los altos valles, desde cuándo? Desde cuándo traemos por dentro es te panorama sutil, tan duro de fundar? Tomé el jolongo mío, y tú tomaste el tuyo, y nos fuimos a ver de cerca al alto valle de las cálidas espigas, de las gruesas ubres, de los aires de cristal: nos fuimos, viéndolo flotante ante los ojos, y nos volvimos hacia la excesiva lluvia y el demasiado polvo.

5. No quisimos detenernos en ir contemplando los valles que alza cada uno; es muy difícil, hay que entrar en sitios sólidos, de manigua cerrada, con muchas escarapelas y permisos. Por recóndito que fuese íbamos a dar al valle de todos, que es el poderoso lente donde convergen las espigas y los caballos en una robusta asociación de silencio y abundancia.

XIII

1. Fierce traffic of ferocities, mine of endings, arena of opposing bodies closing on each other. Ankle stuck persistently, waist blocked, muscle constricted for the leap with the sword, the trident, the scales in hand. Solid cloud of dust that crosses to the wolf, descends to the hyena, rises to the sparrowhawk.

2. But above, in the center, in the cloud that accompanies the man like a vaporous circle, other horizons: earths that in his eyes take on a new clarity and course, as in the first times; that float through the stalks toward the lofted roundness of fruit, like an open hand.

3. Rings of freshness where the hands know themselves through touch and voices, greeting and singing like heavenly mocking-birds; channels of fluid brilliance where the children go down to sail their tacking ships; carved windows, marriage's fragrances, where the maidens of the spirit stretch their fingers of perfume.

4. The dream of the high valleys, for how long? How long have we been bringing this subtle panorama inside, so hard to establish? I took my bag, and you took yours, and we went to see for ourselves the high valley of warm grain, the large udders, the crystal air: we went, watching it float before our eyes, and we went back toward the flood-rains and excess of dust.

5. We didn't want to stop contemplating the valleys that lifted each of us; it's difficult, having to enter fortified places, closed country, with all the insignias and permits. Recondite as it was, we were going to give the valley everything, that slow power where the stalks and horses meet, a strong melding of abundance and silence.

6. En las noches de impotencia, bajo la humedad y la tos, sentados sobre el sillón del desamparo, con el ábaco triste en la mano, nos hemos acordado del valle y la palabra honda que nos hemos dado, como un abierto compromiso. Nos hemos acordado sabiendo que un día de los días será el día, pues, de otro modo, cómo es posible?

7. Vinieron a verme algunos con sus lentes de estaño dormidos sobre el precepto, a ver qué pasa con la luz? Me decían: Ya ha llegado el reino de la luz. Incluso vino uno a quien se le veía la sombra hasta la cintura, así iba el infortunado. Pero recitaba: Ya ha llegado el reino de la luz.

8. Yo me he parado en varios quicios a decir mi canto que va con los tobillos del ensombrecido, para que él identifique sus sombras; y con la sien del vislumbrado, para que él persiga con fuerza la luz. El reino es de la luz, pero no ha sido consumado. Aún crece la albufera de la sombra. Mi canto echa brasa en el corazón dejando la sed sin pausas de la lumbre.

9. Con el primer despunte un día de los días entraremos en la gran ciudad; será con el primer despunte, dentro de una aglomeración juiciosa que conozca bien los pelos del dolor. Así después de sudar nocturnos por los caminos más apretados e irregulares entraremos en la gran ciudad, como bajada del cielo, que nos esperará trinante de pájaros y banderas.

10. Sabes tú de dónde viene? De nuestra penumbra, de la estrechura y la congoja. En el instante terrible de la pérdida la ciudad iba cuajando en lo invisible; dentro del espantoso desaliento, como una paradójica perla, la ciudad crecía con sus terrazas abiertas.

6. In the helpless nights, under the humidity and coughing, sitting in the chair of futility, the forlorn abacus in hand, we have remembered the valley and the deep word we've given ourselves, like an open commitment. We've remembered knowing that one day of days will be the day, otherwise how is it possible?

7. There were some who came to see me with their tin lenses asleep over their precept, to see: what's happening with the light? They were saying to me: The reign of light has already arrived. There was one among them who could be seen shadowed to the waist, the unfortunate one. Still he was reciting: The reign of light has already arrived.

8. I have paused in various doorways to say my song that goes with the ankles of the darkened, so that he might know his shadows; with the temple of the glimpsed, that he might pursue the light with force. The reign is of light, but incomplete. The lagoon of shadow still grows. My song puts coal on the heart that leaves behind the unrelenting thirst of the fire.

9. One day of days, with the first flowering of dawn, we will enter the great city; in the first flowering, within a judicious mass that knows well the strands of pain. Thus after the nightsweats along the most cramped and crooked roads we will enter the great city, as if lowered from the sky, which will wait for us trilling with birds and banners.

10. You know where you come from? From our penumbra, from the dire straits and the distress. In the terrible moment of loss the city was shaping itself in the invisible; within the sudden dismay, like a paradoxical pearl, the city grew with its open terraces.

11. Ya he visto lo que somos, y no pierdo el hilo: todo se presupone y cabe dentro del tramo de sangre que somos; y entonces si se suman bien los tramos nace la magnitud donde es posible la luz.

12. Arriba está el sol, y hacia él hemos de ir: él es una puerta, la mayor que existe, y atravesando los estratos cerrados de la sombra y las aglutinaciones excesivas de la luz, alcanzaremos la más justa eufonía de la sangre.

La Guérnica, 1997

11. I have seen what we are, and not lost the thread: everything is presupposed and fits within the stretch of blood that we are; then if those stretches are added together well, that magnitude is born in which light is possible.

12. Above us is the sun, and toward it we must go: it is one door, the greatest there is, and crossing those closed strata of the dark and the overabundant accretions of light, we will reach the most just euphony of the blood.

Guernica, 1997

INTERVIEWS

What is presented here as a single interview is a selection from an interview of my own and from others conducted by María Antonia Borroto Trujillo, Alejandro Montecinos Larrosa, and Rogelio Riverón, used with permission and with the translator's thanks.

—SR

How did Roberto Manzano know, if there was a time when he knew it, that he would be a poet?

That's something nobody knows. I have my doubts still. What one feels is a vocation, an abiding interest in some activity—in my case, in the world of artistic creation, since painting was what I did first. I had to give up painting because, unlike literature, which a boy can do with a pen and a notebook, even though he doesn't know what comes of those texts after, the painter needs more, and when I was a boy there weren't the resources to develop that vocation fully.

What age would that be?

Around nine, perhaps. I not only did drawings but also made my own toy weapons. I copied the rifles of people in comics and carved them from wood, worked in detail, that is, employing certain principles of sculpture. I earned a certain renown among the boys of that neighborhood for those weapons and sketches. I also was drawn to books, including history and the biographies of great figures. I was especially interested in significant fates, people with some fixed vocation or specific goal: lives outside of the common.

In literature I began with a work that had the typical ingredients of juvenile fiction. I wrote it when I was twelve or thirteen, in Minas de Frío in 1963, and sent it, illustrated, to my parents. It was about a ship's captain who rescued a maiden who was being held hostage on another ship: a love story in the world of pirates.

My primary schooling was very special: I went to preschool in a public school, then to a private school in the neighborhood up to the fourth grade, and after, in the country—the Revolution had not been won yet—I went on a horse with an older friend, the school being far away. When the Revolution triumphed, I went to a school that had already the name of a martyr. I won first place there in a local contest with a drawing of Fidel smoking, and in the smoke haze there was the shape of Jesús Menéndez [1911-1948; famous labor leader in Cuba] with plantations behind him. It was the one time I experienced success: my companions made a big ring around me and tossed me in the air a few times. Through art I had many gratifying experiences.

During my Military Service I was drawing, too, but my muse had little to do with the logistical designs I was supposed to make. At the first opportunity I ran off and drew other things, which cost me a serious reprimand and I was put in a security battalion where I had to be on duty permanently. In Minas de Frío I was doing drawing and poetry at the same time: I was making notes on the natural life of the area.

I was the family's Christmas card specialist. I sent everyone cards made entirely on my own. I never should have let that custom drop; it's interesting to send cards you've made yourself. Later I saw with pleasure how Alberti, Lorca and other great ones made a habit of sending their own hand-made cards.

Cards that have a double value.

Yes, they're kept with greater affection. Little by little the painter was losing ground and the poet gaining force. Already in Tope de Collantes I had many poems I dared to show to others. I remember a companion, older than me and with a certain amount of culture, asking me why they were so sad. At the time, that made me feel awkward about showing them any more. And they weren't sad; I understood later that they had a tenor, a certain romantic character, confessional, that didn't fit the emotional tone of that period, in which epic events dominated, the affirmation of the desire for collective integration. Individual confessions, intimacies, emotions, seemed tonally absurd, belonging to a supposedly superseded romanticism.

Since I had to overcome a natural timidity to show anyone my poems, which are always personally agonizing, I knew to what degree a person could be wounded who showed us his work and we did not respect it with complete human sensibility. For that reason many people have shown me their writings. Someone who gives a poem displays their soul, a piece of their soul. One has to be very careful to protect that. It's an enormous act of confidence, of which one must be worthy. People, young and old alike, that would never share their poems with anyone, have showed them to me. The way I treat others comes from my own experience.

I can't help but notice the presence in your work of many references to the circularity of the universe. Also, in a conversation among friends, you said that the poem is a circularity. Is that circularity the consequence of its existing in nature, something that a country person would know better than anyone?

The circle is the most perfect shape. Between a cube, a pyramid, and a sphere of equal volume, the sphere has greater mass. The sphere, too, is a symbol of the macro-realm, of distance. As the planet stretches away, it rounds. It's also a symbol of the micro-world: as one penetrates more toward the interior, structures more and more spherical are found. Woman, the most beautiful being in the Universe, is described in terms of spheres. When people say their thinking has shape and structure, they say it is well rounded.

Everything in nature occurs cyclically. We discover this more and more: physical cycles, biological, and even economic theories are described in cycles. In the experience of a man close to nature, it's something obvious.

The only thing that can be represented—that is, presented-again—is what already exists, so that the poem represents the universe. The poem is nothing else but a space where a cosmos is attempted. It can succeed or no. If this cosmos is achieved in the space that is the poem, then no element can be extracted from it because that disrupts its ecology: not even a comma can be dispensed with, because it disrupts the ecosystem. A poem is a system with a marvelous ecology. Sometimes interpretive theories, the moment they're applied concretely to a poem, go wrong because they forget this metaphor of the cosmos. A poem is a cosmos and as such its laws must be applied.

One of the first of those is that the poem is constructed in the same way as the great metaphor of Genesis. The creative act is represented by a traditional gesture: the invention of light. That's simply the passage from disorder to order, from entropy to synergy. Where there is chaos, there is no love. Love is synergy, embrace, circle. We come back to the circle. My poetry tries to retain all the physical-material properties of the world. It works to construct a metaphor to serve as the obverse of physical laws, which might appear to clip the wings of the imagination, but no. For example, I never transgress against the motions of light and gravity. I know that in the imagination there are fixed laws that are the counterparts of the physical ones: precisely by being their opposites they are similar. The opposite, the most opposed thing on the scale, is united through analogy. In the long run everything ends up being the same. What happens is that it's perceived as opposite because there's some certain immediate disjunction, but when seen from sufficient distance the diverse appears as one. García Márquez shows that with the myth of the old Buendía tied to the tree, the old Buendía who at that stage of his life had as his one companion the very man that he had killed. His enemy accompanies him. There is no companion like one's enemy, which again reflects the idea of the circle.

The same thing occurs in a poem: all extremes are united, because it bears the greatest possible rationality. It is subject to the laws of the exterior world. In the poem objective and subjective are united, rational and emotional, collective and individual. The poem resolves antimonies, false dichotomies: the poem is what unifies, the absolute unity: the cosmos. In the cosmos this is all included. This is why the building of a poem brings such joy, like constructing a world. It's the one chance to do this, since we come to a world that's already made. The poem is the chance to be God, to be the demiurge, the maker of a world. That world should come from the very core of the poet.

And yes, the idea of gender is there in the creative instant, too. But something exists there that is transgender, transsexual, I don't know what to call it, in which the creator is child, old person, man, woman, white, black. What today, in our divided culture, creates segregations, peripheries, marginalized territories, is resolved. When the poet speaks and his word is authentic, all that disappears. In the voice expressed there, which is not exactly the physical voice of the person who made the poem, all the contradictions are resolved that had seemed insuperable. Goethe said, in *Conversations with Eckermann*, that in the poet are all sexes, races, and ages. The greatness of some poets lies in the immense multitude lined up behind their little I. The poem is a gnostic space in which impasses are broken, and the universe holds together.

One finds in your poetry the use of terms belonging to science, which goes against the myth that poetry is written only with certain kinds of words.

Poets love their paradigms. We devote ourselves to many illusory affirmations in order to defend our business. We've struggled with this from antiquity because the act of creation is seen as something inspired, intuitive, mysterious, ineffable; something unavailable to human rationality; that has to be accepted as incomprehensible.

Another of these paradigms is that reason can't sing, that what sings is the heart, emotion, sentiment, fancy, intuition, premonition. When people defend reason's capacity to sing, they're quickly contradicted. I believe that where the results are most pure and beautiful, the intelligence is there. The interconnection of the sexes without intellect is very sad and approaches the domain of pure instinct. Whatever belongs to the realm of the animal must be added to: man is explained by what he adds. Martí said: A step is heard beyond what rises in shadow. Man is what is added with this new step. The poet is a being that makes new additions. From the start the word poetry has meant invention, addition, discovery: if there is nothing added, there is no poetry. The intelligence plays an extraordinary role in this act of adding-on: the instincts, the emotions, the affections have origins that are highly spontaneous and flow in a way that makes it hard to construct a poem from only those materials. The writer must, then, select. Insofar as the individual takes on this role of selecting, the intelligence is present: that role marks the difference. Machado said: Poet, steady as you go. It implies an attitude of selection, discrimination, of the rational component for presenting the most uncontrolled of emotions. Martí said that to write is to choose, and Simón Bolivar that haste is a crime for the poet. The poem is always presented as an immediate act performed with one emotional frequency, but this is a false paradigm: the real poem is made with emotional memory: what writes the poem is emotional memory, which is why the lyric has this evocative, nostalgic, yearning character, though it is in the present. In my view rationality, too, has the secret of dreams.

Science always seems to be where absolute rationality reigns. But many aesthetic elements are found in it. A well-finished equation is beautiful. Einstein's on energy is absolutely beautiful. One way of validating an equation is its aesthetic result: if it isn't elegant it's because there is some unresolved contradiction. From a humanistic perspective of man, the scientific has nothing to fear from the aesthetic, and the aesthetic from the scientific. At the end of the day man is the measure of things. Science and poetry are nothing more than manifestations of man's integrated nature. There are two cerebral hemispheres, but our thought occurs as a unity.

To what poets do you feel closest?

Many. I've always changed preferences. One of the first I read was Martí. I learned from Martí early on that the best way to defend oneself from the tyranny of a model is to read a variety of literatures. That's lead me to have many teachers and influences at once.

Picasso, who was a writer, too, left us many valuable teachings. The first is that if a creator wants to have an extended working span, he must continually devour himself and be reborn: cyclically, he has to achieve this sacrifice of himself. A great creator kills himself off periodically, in order to revive later. Creators who are one bright flash, whose work is not sustained, are creators of another type, since they find it very difficult to form cycles of creation: they dive in quickly, wholly, and almost in their final form from the start. They don't fulfill the myth of Osiris. They don't follow nature. But the vast majority of creators do. Picasso died every now and then and was reborn. He kept being Picasso, but different at the same time. Creators who keep writing into their later years have that secret: the secret of knowing how to die and be reborn: the secret of the pendulum. Martí was of that sort, though through his public service and his own poetic mandate he ended up dying when he was scarcely 42.

I have dreamt for myself something like this as a creative process; but I don't know if I've succeeded in applying it.

To know great writers personally is always a formidable thing, but sometimes more is learned through direct contact with their work: but one has to guess the process from the result, since art shows us results, and doesn't like to show the hardship its costs to get a noble result.

I remember one time I was able to have a conversation with Guillén. But still, my most fruitful conversation was with his work. That's where I learned about artistic care, respect for the language, experiencing my daily traditions, not blinding myself with fashions.

In art, sometimes the most graceful forms, like a bull of Picasso's that he drew with a single line, can cost forty-five days of work. A printer that worked with him used to complain how he would begin with this magnificent bull, one that anyone would envy, then each time take off more flesh until he was left with a bull in word only, emotional, abstract: the bull that he was dreaming. It's incredible the number of sketches he had to make in order to achieve the perfection of Guernica, for example.

In poetry it's very difficult to show the creative process. I only know of one case in Cuban poetry, a poem of Guillén's, in which the poem, made of five or six stanzas that alter very few words, demonstrates the journey from its beginning to the end. The completed work is the process itself.

I incorporate into my work the experiences and practices of other creators. What has happened to one creator of whatever sort is interesting, it teaches, it educates: from that point of view many creators have influenced me.

Writing about *Song to the Savannah*, **your first book, Rafael Almanza says that "with this book begins the lyric reaction that supplants colloquialism." Can you explain that by describing the literary atmosphere in which your first book appeared?**

This is about the process of Cuban literary history. This process tends to involve advances that follow one after the other, where one movement is substituted for another—this happens everywhere. In the sixties in Cuba, owing to very particular historical circumstances, there was a tendency to move away from metaphor and other more refined modes of literary expression and use more colloquial, familiar modes of everyday Cuban speech. It rejected classical formal notions like meter and forms like the sonnet, the décima, the quantities and rhythms traditionally associated with Spanish, and used the language of everyday life, including newspapers and political slogans; it was very much influenced by North American poetry, including Pound and Eliot in some respects, and it became very influential in Latin America in the sixties. But as soon as the cultural situation changes one finds that this approach changes along with it, and by the beginning of the seventies it was plain that this was a kind of rhetoric only and that it had to be transformed. In literature you can more or less predict some of these changes—you can ask a literary group what they are not doing, and it becomes the thing that the next generation will take up. In the seventies—this is back when I was in my twenties—there were many of us who did not want to write in this manner, but rather in a more polished style, something sonorous and with elegance, that recuperated the old resources of the language and, faced with the urban world, expressed our rural origins. *Song to the Savannah* is a reflection of this new interest among us.

In that book, and in many of your poems, you often use distance and travel as metaphors. One poem describes the distance as "an endlessness flags that signal and obligate." What is the traveler in your poems usually seeking? What are those flags, and what obligations do they impose?

You've chosen a very appropriate image for discussing my work. To my mind, poetry that is universal starts from three or four basic imaginative "cells," so to speak. Poets create infinite combinations of things and present an extremely rich image, but the essential, constructive elements are few. One of these is the struggle that exists between light and shadow, for which human beings have a special sensibility and which is continually being converted into symbols. The light represents joy, freedom, family, truth; and the shadow an absence of these, oblivion, a whole range of things; and the poet is always moving from light to shadow, from shadow to light, like part of a binary system. It's something to which literary criticism has perhaps not paid sufficient attention. When the poet speaks of happiness he suddenly finds himself in these luminous spaces at the level of language, and when he speaks of its opposite he finds himself articulating a whole different imaginative terrain. The tree is another such symbol—of roots, growth, bearing fruit; these things are found everywhere in universal poetry, and many cultures have the tree as a central symbol of life; and the road, too, the traveler, the goal, wanderings, this too is a central image. In the line to which you refer, we are talking about symbols of human destiny, the species as a whole; each nation calls its people to the journey, toward what's ahead, toward questions that have not yet been answered, and these goals, of whatever sort they might be, are the flags that accompany us on the way.

A number of people—writers, mostly—have commented very positively on the way in which you employ abstraction, like soul, spirit, universe, love. It's something that's not common in poetry in the United States, really; in fact we teach people to be wary of abstractions and rely on the specific image to reflect emotion. Does this feature attract the attention of a Cuban audience as well? Or does it speak to a different cultural sensibility?

Yes, a Cuban audience would notice that, in the sense that the poetry most frequently come across, the work of my contemporaries, I mean, has something anecdotal behind it that refers to a very particular, localized situation. That's how their way of proceeding works, and I think it's a valid method. But there's something in me—not only in my view of the universe but in my aesthetic sensibilities, that makes me reach for a range of metaphor that is all-embracing, I am aware of that. I have a great love of popular, spoken poetry, because in peoples who have no writing, about whom I have read a lot and in whom I take a great interest, these metaphoric, cosmic leaps are quite common, because their sensibility was such that the totality of the cosmos and the "I" were a unity. And I tend constantly to integrate myself into the cosmos. As in my book *Clay Tablets*, I like to combine contemporary and ancient sensibilities, the individual and the collective, fusing these things together, which is, too, what *Synergos* is all about. Of course, I was not aware of all this at the beginning of my development. It seems to me that in North American poetry—and this is a subjective opinion since I lack knowledge in this area—but in the North American poetry I have seen there has been a turning away from the all-embracing vision of a poet like Whitman.

Can you discuss your sense of how your influences work in

your creative system—because they're quite varied, from Saint-John Perse to Whitman. How does this come to be?

When it is taking shape, the poetic world is very agglutinative; it selects from scattered possibilities and establishes what it selects in its very core, precisely because it is in a state of formation, and all the elements enter into the nucleus to shape the world that is being created. What I saw as especially appealing in Whitman was the sense of the elements, the cosmic plurality, the earthly infinitude, the attitude of celebration, the embodiment of the great spiritual motions of the individual that break off spiraling toward the universal. I admired that in Whitman. Other things I discarded: for example, his very long lists, which I had seen already in the conversational poetry of my time, and which didn't seem sufficiently promising for a language of lyric synthesis. Later I heard that the colloquialists had read a lot of Whitman, and Eliot and Pound, and North American literature generally. But the Whitman I read is not the one they read, though the text is the same. I don't attend to the lists, those profuse and slow catalogues of sensations or objects, which suggest the multi-faceted gaze and the tremendous plurality of what surrounds him, which Neruda employed so well but which was so impoverished in the hands the colloquial Cuban and Latin American writers with their smaller angle of vision, and which was the natural legacy of North American poetry of the 70s; it didn't enter in to my system of appropriation precisely as a rejection of what colloquialism employed as peculiarly their own and as one of the basic resources for emphasizing the spoken character of their discourse. The attitude of celebration, of welcoming disparate things, of what creation produces from chaos, of the dignity of all things, the sense that everything is important, that everyone has the right to be part of the song, that everyone is capable of giving, offering, creating: that vision takes its shape in me in an artistic way, not philosophical, through Whitman. From Saint-John Perse comes the capacity for metaphoric growth, transforming a naked space into the ground of allusion, the tendency toward suggestion and obliquity in the message. The underlying sense of a drama behind the song that creates a bottomless, inexhaustible lyric, and the argument giving shape to the emotion from the depths, where the exact body of the poem can't be made out behind the dead leaves, the horses in water, telluric images that Perse handles so well, whose texts have a tropical and symbolic density that really comes from the imaginative sensibility of the Carribean. And I am with Martí in deciding that the I has the right to sing for the entire universe, whenever the I is present, it is offered to that whole world, whenever there exists a symbiosis of generosity, good will, interchange, of reconciling between what man sees as apparently a dichotomy, divided in two. The subjective can express the most disembodied objectivity. The I can express country, homeland, all of humanity. Furthermore, the extraordinary use of metaphor, the expressive resources as fluid and incandescent, the shining interior in what is said, the sense of unmistakable elegance in his writing, opposed always to clumsiness, to carelessness, lack of solidity, of surprises, of synthesis, all that I admire in Martí: it's very appealing from an artistic point of view, and it enters my aesthetic consciousness as a kind of underlying objective. Not that I've achieved that ever, but it's what I always look for there. There, elsewhere, in the other, then another, where I come to know a little what I am and what I want to be: only through this purposeful appropriation. Each poet chooses his roads, and enters into various dwellings, and returns with different harvests from the same traveled fields. I could continue detailing this process, but you should know the following, too: it's not just on poets that the poet thrives, because there are many fiction writers that have also influenced me heavily. Reading Rulfo [Juan Rulfo, 1917-1986, Mexican fiction writer], for example, is unforgettable. Sometimes those dead figures in Rulfo, or his poor people walking through a plain in the middle of suffocating heat, they're in my poetry, too, but transmuted, treated in accordance with my expressive needs, made to belong more properly to my world and my communicative intent.

Are you a monumentalist?

I love the monumental. The great frescoes, the great murals. I love very much the Greek bas-relief, the grand facades, where over the space of meters and meters an artist outlines a whole world, a series and sequence of bodies in various positions and situations, in variations, in growth. I like the great spirals, the movement of waves when they reach shoreline. I like the great open spaces that have long stretches of horizon. I like works that have not only material weight but spiritual, too. Works that weigh as much from the physical perspective as from the mental, without dichotomy, they fascinate me, and if I had the talent, the life, the time and resources, I would dream of making structures of that sort. My desire would be to write as the sea writes, as the great elements of nature write. There's a phrase of Neruda's that I subscribe to: I would devour it all, include it all in my song, I would put it there as in an amazing cup, like a Greek cornucopia of abundance, like those images that in world culture present the idea that everything is gathered together, stitched together, united. This is what I, with my temperament, would like to do, what I would dream of doing. But here's something to consider. I am the child of laborers, of country people, and I'm going to say something that's a little daring in this time when it's not fashionable to speak of classes, or of class instinct, or the linkings of class to art or to the psychological phenomena of creation, that seems too much: but I would dare to say that the man who works and the man who has, all his life, been in contact with the natural, primary world through his work, tends spiritually to love the monumental. I don't mean that he isn't fascinated before a little miniature jewel case, before a work of Benvenuto Cellini's, who as Martí said put Jupiter in a salt cellar. Before that stupendous salt cellar, which is a work of genius and of human creation, any person regardless of class is dazzled. But, and I don't know why, I sense that the man who is closer to the natural, that deals continually and mysteriously with the primordial substances, that works with sand, with bone, with wood, with mud, through strange associative mechanisms, loves the cosmic; and the cosmic is frightening, it's terrible, not only due to its size but because of the idea of its internal design.

Synergos, **which won Cuba's highest literary prize, seems to me**

monumental in this sense. Could you discuss the design of those poems, the configuration of the line, which seems different from anything you'd done before?

Synergos attempts to suit its contents to its formal dimension. First of all, the lines are open forms, not written in any regular rhythm at all, but they have their expressive limits. Each expressive unit closes with a semi-colon, which suggests a rupture but at the same time a continuity, so that the text proceeds, goes forward continually, without capitals, since the capitals indicate a new beginning, whereas the text wants to be fluid and continuous. A statement, then a silence, a statement, then a silence, in a series, a sequence, a linear progression, which is the way I think of time. So that's the philosophy behind the form, since the poet has to present his material in such a way that its shape is part of the message.

What kind of break does *Synergos* represent with the work that precedes it.

None. *Synergos* is of a piece with what comes before, both in content and form. The search for centrality in the world, the aspiration that it be coordinated and interconnected by the highest of aims, the urgent need of the embrace in a world that staggers forward like someone who's been shot, these are currents in my thought that comes from earlier work to *Synergos* and form an inextricable part of my poetry's deepest and most permanent messages. It's just that *Synergos* takes them up more fully and with an imaginative configuration that's more exact. But it's true to say that the book is another moment, a distinct instant in my poetic evolution, since it seems to me to have achieved a certain maturity in the use of the verse form, which I was using more and more frequently, as one of the promising resources of contemporary lyric expression. Though there are, too, in the whole, as part of the synergistic spirit that governs it, formal elements that run from the distich, that ancient strophe, to certain reconfigurations of the décima. So as you can you see, *Synergos* is both a creation in transition and a finished thing, as really any artistic product is.

What importance, of whatever kind, does something like the Nicholás Guillén Prize have?

According to the established institutional hierarchy, it's the highest prize for poetry in Cuba today. But let's not forget that it's only a contest, it's worth saying, and that it has all the defects and virtues of this controversial element of literary life. But, okay, this isn't the time for analysis, but rather celebration.

How does a poet react when he goes to bed a mere mortal and wakes up to discover he's won a great prize?

With the happiness of one who's suddenly been favored by good fortune. Because it's really just a morsel of good luck that should be savored with all the simplicity in the world, like any widely longed-for sustenance that one receives unexpectedly. Three people constitute a panel of judges, the book that you have previously sent is put forward, some expertise in the contest in which you are participating, a certain consensus to act impartially and fairly, and there you are: this is how you end up with a prize. Joy in being selected, gratitude for the selectors, a blessing for those creators who tend to the required details and end up being honored, without any despotic affiliations.

—SR

Books from Etruscan Press

Legible Heavens | H. L. Hix

A Poetics of Hiroshima | William Heyen

Saint Joe's Passion | J. D. Schraffenberger

American Fugue | Alexis Stamtais

Drift Ice | Jennifer Atkinson

The Widening | Carol Moldaw

Parallel Lives | Michael Lind

God Bless: A Political/Poetic Discourse | H. L. Hix

Chromatic | H. L. Hix (National Book Award finalist)

The Confessions of Doc Williams & Other Poems | William Heyen

Art into Life | Frederick R. Karl

Shadows of Houses | H. L. Hix

The White Horse: A Colombian Journey | Diane Thiel

Wild and Whirling Words: A Poetic Conversation | H. L. Hix

Shoah Train | William Heyen (National Book Award finalist)

Crow Man | Tom Bailey

As Easy As Lying: Essays on Poetry | H. L. Hix

Cinder | Bruce Bond

Free Concert: New and Selected Poems | Milton Kessler

September 11, 2001: American Writers Respond | William Heyen

etruscan press
www.etruscanpress.org

Etruscan Press books may be ordered from:

Consortium Book Sales and Distribution
800-283-3572
www.cbsd.com

Small Press Distribution
800-869-7553
www.spdbooks.com